To eat is a necessity,
but to eat intelligently is an art.

— Francois de La Rochefoucauld, 1613-1680

The smallest things make the biggest difference.®

Smart Weight Loss

Change your body

Change your mind

Ray Haring, Ph.D.

HealthSpan COMMUNICATIONS®

Acknowledgments

*To my family, friends, and those who understand
that joy, love, and peace are life's greatest treasures.*

*My sincerest appreciation and special thanks are extended
to Gay Carroll and Elena Macaluso for their editorial assistance.*

*Graphic design: Ellen Baxter in association
with HealthSpan Communications®*

Publisher's Note to the Reader

This book was not written to serve as an all-encompassing manual on diet, exercise, and weight management. Rather, this book was designed to augment the reader's understanding of basic principles of weight management and to encourage the reader to further his or her knowledge by reading and studying additional publications in the field that are supported and approved by the scientific and medical communities.

First Edition, 2007

Library of Congress Catalog Card Number 2006925605
ISBN-10: 1-59470-100-8
ISBN-13: 978-1-59470-100-9
UPC: 690861990024

www.smallest*things*.com
email: healthspan@smallestthings.com

PRINTED IN THE UNITED STATES OF AMERICA

*"No one has ever lost weight
by depriving themselves of knowledge."*

Introduction

This book celebrates the miracle of how the smallest things can make the biggest differences in our physical, emotional, and spiritual well-being.

As you explore the thoughts and messages expressed in the pages to come, I hope you will be touched, inspired, and enlightened.

It is also my hope that you come to appreciate that the smallest things that you see or don't see—believe or don't believe—do or don't do—will make the biggest difference in the direction of your life.

To your health.
Best always,

Raymond V. Haring, Ph.D.
President, HealthSpan Communications®

Contents

Contents

Contents

Contents

Contents

Eat Like Socrates

The rest of the world lives to eat,
while I eat to live.

— Socrates, 470-399 B.C.

Eat To Live

Some of the most brilliant ideas and philosophies need little, if any, explanation. Of the many different principles or tenets by which we live our lives, there's one school of thought dealing with nutrition that is universally accepted by virtually all health care providers.

The doctrine is simple: "Eat to live—don't live to eat."

Honestly, give it a try.

It works wonders.

When it involves nourishment, best is better than good.

So, go for the best!

Live life.

And eat to live.

As you read and explore the ideas in this book, you will discover that the science and philosophy behind the concept of "Smart Weight Loss" has as much to do with encouraging a healthy lifestyle, as it does with helping you shed unwanted pounds.

Losing pounds is one thing.

Losing pounds and promoting health through healthy lifestyle choices is quite another thing.

The power of simply understanding that the smallest things you do or don't do, eat or don't eat, will make the biggest difference in the success of your efforts.

So, here's to life.

And to your good health.

Eat to live.

Food For Thought

The wisest mind has something yet to learn.

— George Santayana, 1863-1952

Feed Your Brain First

Let's be blunt.

No one has ever lost weight by depriving themselves of knowledge. What you put in your brain is just as important as what you put in your mouth. Educating yourself as to the nutritional value of foods and snacks and the importance of leading a healthy lifestyle is a necessary first step toward inproving your diet, increasing your level of physical fitness, and enhancing your health.

Read.

Learn.

Think.

Choose.

Then eat.

Our brains need to be fed information long before our stomachs are fed any food. When you consider how difficult it is to think on an empty stomach, you will appreciate how difficult it is to make healthy decisions when your brain isn't full of healthful facts and useful tips.

With a little study and rehearsal, the learning process will become automated and your choices and decisions will become automatic.

In short order, healthy habits will supplant the need for perpetual study. You will just intuitively know what to eat and what not to eat.

In the meantime, here's a little food for thought.

Where should you shop for brain food?

The American Medical Association.

The American Dietetics Association.

The American Heart Association.

The American Cancer Society.

The U.S. Food and Drug Administration.

The American College of Sports Medicine.

This menu should whet your appetite for awhile.

Catch-Up

No—I'm not talking about ketchup.

I'm talking about doing little things to keep yourself current with the latest news and information on a wide variety of health and diet related topics.

Traditionally, libraries and bookstores have been great places to spend spare time relaxing, browsing, and catching up on favorite authors and books.

With the widespread use of personal computers and the advent of the worldwide Internet, many people today are instantly getting their information conveniently displayed on their computer screens directly in front of them.

The use of personal computers to access information is one of the quickest ways to catch up on the latest news releases and scientific discoveries.

Whether you're doing some major research or doing some minor brushing up on health related topics, it's always important to first ask a few questions about the material you're about to read.

Who is the author?

Who supports the author? Who doesn't?

What credentials and degrees does the author hold?

Has the author's publications or research been called into question by the scientific or medical community?

Is the author's intent to educate the public or is the author just trying to sell something?

Stay informed.

Stay current.

Catch-up!

The Skinny on Round and Square Meals

No wonder people are confused about diets.
Sometimes they're told their diet should be round.
Sometimes square.
What's a person to do?
And what's a balanced diet? Does that mean you should eat equal portions of all the foods you get in your diet?
No.
That kind of diet would be imbalanced. And what about the suggestion that you, "eat everything in moderation."
No again.
My first question is, "what's 'everything'?"
Who knows!
Secondly, the word "moderation" is just too vague.
The problem with all this "advice" is that it doesn't help you make the best nutritional decisions.
Vague ideas produce nebulous and ambiguous results. And ambiguous results lead to confusion and uncertainty.
So, as you read this book, or any book or article for that matter, I encourage you to pay close attention to any new ideas that challenge or call into question your original understanding of a concept.
There is no substitute for accurate, detailed information when it comes to learning about your diet and health.
So, strengthen your vocabulary.
Bolster your knowledge.
Benefit from your wisdom.
In no time you will be using more descriptive words like, "nutritionally dense foods," rather than "square or round" to describe the meals that make up your diet.

Heads-Up

"One of the most important considerations before starting a diet is to know whether the medical and scientific community supports the dietary program or product."

Who's on First?

"Always eat this. Never eat that."
"Eat this only after you eat that."
"Drink this 30 minutes before you eat that."
Do these regimens sound too familiar or at best a bit nonsensical in their demands? Are you a bit confused about all the different diets and weight loss programs? There appears to be no end to programs that promote pills, potions, and promises for weight loss and a new, slimmer you.

Startling discoveries about new weight loss techniques that sporadically make *headlines* can be confusing, costly, and potentially dangerous—especially for people seeking nonmedical weight loss solutions from unproven remedies or unscrupulous schemes.

There are countless commercials and advertisements touting viewpoints with unsubstantiated claims or foundations. Until some *new* diet or eating regimen is proven valid, medical and scientific consensus likely will not support recommendations for their use in the field of weight management. It does not make sense to risk potential health problems by subscribing to or adopting the "latest and greatest" unsubstantiated fad diet.

One of the most important considerations before starting a diet is to know whether the medical and scientific community supports the dietary program or product.

When you start paying closer attention to who's pitching to you, you will be much smarter about taking wild swings at curve balls tossed your way.

Get informed before you go to bat.

And remember, heads-up!

Think Again

The cautious seldom err.

— Confucius, 551-479 B.C.

Exercise Caution

Exercise. Exercise. Exercise.

Like most of us, you're probably reminded daily of this message by someone special in your life.

Generally, this is a good thing. Our loved ones are just trying to tell us, in their own way, that they care for us.

Okay.

Today, you're not going to take their advice and exercise. Instead, you're going to just think about exercising. In fact you're going to exercise something other than your muscles.

Your muscles get the day off.

Today, I want you to exercise some "caution." Sometimes it's just as important to exercise caution as it is to exercise your body or mind.

So, when should you exercise *caution*?

The simple answer is often.

The longer answer is, if for any reason you're considering the use of any gadgets, gimmicks, drugs, or medications to help you lose weight, then you NEED to thoroughly discuss this issue with your physician.

I strongly believe that ONLY licensed physicians or medical doctors should be the individuals responsible for advising people about health, diet, and exercise and whether to use medications or drugs in a weight loss program.

For extra vigilance and caution, you may even want to get a second or third opinion from additional doctors in the medical field.

Again, I strongly encourage you to often remind yourself to ALWAYS first consult with your physician regarding any and all aspects of your health and when considering making changes to any aspect of your diet or exercise program.

Remember, you don't always have to exercise your muscles; but, you should always exercise caution.

Be cautious. Be safe. Be healthy.

Change Tomorrow by Changing Today

*"Start changing tomorrow
. . . by changing today."*

The Past Doesn't Equal the Future

It's true.

The future can be very different from the past.

For starters, the past is full of memories, and the future, hopefully, is full of wonderful dreams.

Remember, stubborn pounds you've been wearing don't have to be worn tomorrow.

Do you want to lighten up and shed some pounds?

To lose extra weight you may consider losing some extra *baggage* that may have accumulated over the years. Letting go of things that are out-of-date that no longer serve you is one of the quickest and easiest ways to lighten your load. Trashing that all too familiar self-defeating mantra, "I can't lose weight, because I haven't so far," will serve you well.

All of us at one time or another have carried enough counterproductive thoughts in our heads that we may have momentarily felt weighed down.

That's normal.

But, it's when you carry a burdensome load for so long that you begin to feel that your future is held captive by your past, that it's time for you to again hear the message, "The past doesn't equal the future."

Sure, your present condition or weight is based on your past behavior, but future results are based on what you do today, not on what you did yesterday or the day before yesterday.

Just because you have felt something or done something a certain way your entire life doesn't mean you have to continue doing or feeling the same way on into infinitum.

Remember, the extent to which you change your future or shape your body will be determined by what you are willing to do differently today.

So, change tomorrow by first changing today.

Forecast Your Weight

Some people give great credence to the predictions and projections of stargazers and clairvoyant fortune-tellers.

I don't—but that's just me.

I believe quite strongly, however, in predictions that we make about ourselves. These forecasts or predictions are called self-fulfilling prophecies and they work like this: Our belief about something causes us to act or behave in a certain way.

For a moment, imagine yourself as the architect of a self-fulfilling prophecy. For instance, you may initially believe that for whatever reason you can't lose weight; therefore, you don't try. Without trying, nothing happens. When nothing happens, you have all the evidence and proof you need that your self-fulfilling prophecy was accurate.

A self-fulfilling prophecy doesn't have to be a self-defeating prophecy; it can be a constructive self-refreshing prophecy that is positive rather than limiting or self-defeating.

All of us, at one time or another, have made predictions based on past experiences and beliefs. These rather innocuous forecasts will eventually become our reality, simply because we subscribe to certain beliefs.

Your potential to lose weight is reached by believing that you can manage your weight.

If you believe you can't, you won't.

If you believe you can, you will.

So be positive.

The success of your weight management program begins with your next self-refreshing prophecy.

Go ahead—forecast your weight.

What will it be?

Life is a Journey

Whether life is a voyage, odyssey, or adventure, there's one thing for certain—life is not a final destination, but rather a voyage guided by our thoughts and led by our dreams and aspirations.

Each step of our journey is governed by little decisions that we make minute by minute, and day by day.

Like life, your health, happiness, and overall sense of well-being are determined by the quality of your thoughts and actions. Think of decisions as the glue that firmly cements your wishes into commitments rather than obscure dreams.

To the point.

Your weight.

Have you ever experienced any weight fluctuations over the years that seemed more like a roller-coaster ride than a stroll through a park?

You're not alone.

Maintaining your weight is a lifetime journey—not a theme-park ride.

Who wants to lose weight only to gain it back?

No one!

There are two phases to weight loss.

Losing the weight.

And then keeping it from returning.

Period.

Changing your diet and lifestyle confronts both issues. Sure, it would be wonderful to receive a stamped guarantee that keeps weight from returning. Unfortunately, no such certificate exists. As with all things in life, weight, health, and fitness are always subject to change.

With determination, patience, and the zeal for travel, your journey will be an adventure with fewer lumps and bumps.

Support Your Values With Your Full Weight

"A value, unsupported by rules and limits, is like a chair without legs. There is nothing to support your weight."

The Value of Values

What do values have to do with losing weight?

Plenty.

But first, what are values?

Values are principles that you hold in high regard. Simply put, what you value possesses a certain degree of desirability. Consequently, the values you hold dear to your heart will determine the decisions you make, give guidance to the direction of your life, and provide meaning to your pursuits in life.

We all have values.

Some values include good health, a great job, a happy home life, meaningful spare time, close friendships, and sufficient money. While the list goes on, the important point is that the *degree* of desirability determines the relative importance of the value.

Due to time constraints or lack of resources, we are often forced to prioritize our values. For example: Not doing things you think are most important, choosing foods based on taste rather than health, or looking for instant gratification rather than waiting for the grand prize you really desire.

Let's take a little quiz.

What do you value the most?

Cheesecake or a slimmer body?

Greasy food or a healthy heart?

Be careful, a value, unsupported by rules and limits, is like a chair without legs. There is nothing to support your weight.

Consider the person who wants a healthy heart but who still consumes unhealthy foods. *Thinking* about a value is much different than *living* it. If you are unsure about what you value, you need to look at what you are doing or eating.

What you do is what you value.

If overeating plays an unusually significant part in your

life, then food has extra importance or value to you. If a slimmer and fitter body is more important to you than eating extra food or desserts, then health and fitness have more significance or value to you.

The first step in making any change in life is to first develop an awareness of the need to make modifications or revisions to old thinking or counterproductive habits. After the initial wake-up call, then the actual work or commitment period ensues.

This material isn't rocket science, but it is common sense.

Big commitments produce big results.

Weak commitments produce disappointing results.

Valuing health and fitness between eating binges is much like valuing your lungs between smoking breaks.

Nothing is learned.

And nothing is gained.

So, witness your strength.

Embrace your principles and values.

Stand up against temptations that don't serve your best interests. For starters, bid farewell to the old, clingy friends that no longer support your new lifestyle.

Be nice.

And be gentle with your goodbyes.

Say to your old *pals*:

Bon voyage butter rolls.

Bye-bye cream puffs.

So long hot dogs.

Adios ice cream.

See you later potato chips.

Sayonara sausage.

And don't forget to say aloha to the new healthier, slimmer you.

Breeding Grounds For Feeding Frenzies

What does your environment have to do with what you eat, when you eat, and how much you eat?

Plenty.

Your environment or *world* you live in includes not only the physical elements that make up your surroundings, but also the mental, social, and spiritual thoughts that occupy your consciousness. What you see, touch, hear, remember, and understand all contribute to your perception of your environment.

Here is how it works.

Positive or healthy environments produce positive or healthy thinking. Negative or unhealthy environments produce negative or unhealthy thinking. And we all know that for many people, dismal thoughts are breeding grounds for depression and overeating. Certainly, all the candy, cakes, pies, or liquor in the world won't eliminate one negative thought from a person's brain.

As a general rule, if you are not happy with certain aspects of your environment, you need to change them. To change any aspect of your environment, you must first begin by changing your thoughts.

Pure and simple, thoughts are images and ideas that we ponder and process. Never underestimate the power or influence of a single thought. A single thought can make the difference between destroying a life or bringing about enormous success and happiness.

Think positive, and you'll feel positive.

So.

Change your thoughts.

Change your environment.

Change how you feel.

Then you will see how much easier it is to change when, where, what, and how much you eat.

Geniuses Aren't Know-It-Alls

The greatest genius will not be worth much if he
pretends to draw exclusively from his own resources.

— Wolfgang von Goethe, 1749-1832

Two Helpings, Please

Sometimes the phrase, "Monkey see, monkey do," literally scares me. I'm not trying to make any comparison between humans and primates, but it's human nature to acquire certain behaviors by simply watching other people do things.

That's right.

The most basic research has shown that people do as they see, not as they are told.

It's called role modeling.

Yes, it can work for you, and unfortunately at times it can work against you. It just depends on what you're watching, who you're watching, and also the other things you see or visualize in your mind.

Having any doubts about the power of this message?

Well, just hang a large poster of your favorite dessert right next to your desk, and then see how easy it is to take your mind off snacking. Incidentally, visualizing the dessert in detail can be just as effective as a picture—very difficult to get it out of your mind.

So, be careful about the things you watch. What you watch, can sometimes be very difficult to remove from your thoughts.

Occasionally, you may even need a little extra help to get your "head" in a different frame of mind.

There's an old adage that says, "Two heads are better than one." And I'm not talking about two heads of cabbage or lettuce. I'm referring to two people helping each another in very subtle ways.

For instance, you can unwittingly be inspired by simply watching a spirited person be passionate.

Albert Einstein once said, "Setting an example is not the main means of influencing another, it is the only means."

I agree.

This means, however, that you have to be attentive to

whom you are watching. If you want to get in shape, then associate with someone who also seriously wants to get in shape. If you're interested in gaining a few extra pounds, then spend your spare time watching gourmet chefs prepare, cook, and serve delicious foods at a restaurant or on your television set.

Spending too much energy thinking about this concept can be counterproductive and consume too much of your own valuable time. It's now time for you to go looking for a slice of someone else's time. You can accomplish this in a number of different ways without being noticed or obtrusive.

Instead of browsing through cookbooks, trading recipes, or watching someone cook, focus your thoughts on people and things that inspire and encourage you to lose weight. It's just easier to lose weight if you're watching someone else lose weight, rather than trying to lose weight watching someone setting themselves up to gain weight.

Make it easy on yourself.

Give yourself a break.

Here's to two helpings, please!

Mind Over Body

It seems the more we learn about foods, the more questions we ultimately have about them. That's just the way discovery and learning occur. In addition, it just shows you have a curious mind that's searching for more and more answers to more and more questions.

Interestingly, your brain and nervous system burn many calories each day thinking and searching for solutions and answers to your questions.

I must admit, the mere thought of using our brains to lose weight sounds great. But wait, don't get too excited about losing weight by working through those mind-binding crossword puzzles.

Why not?

Well, the answer is simple. It turns out that mindlessly watching grass grow burns approximately the same number of calories as working on a complicated physics problem.

So ultimately, the big question still remains to be answered. Is your brain intimately involved in helping you lose weight?

Absolutely!

But only if you're willing to listen to the signals that your brain is trying to send to you. Here are three of the most common messages that frequently emanate from the deep reaches of our brains: "Get off the couch, put the fork down, and move your body."

Am I right?

I thought so!

Incidentally, these messages are the most often ignored by many of us.

Take charge. Use your mind to direct you and your muscles to move you.

Trust me.

Your muscles won't talk back to you if you're the boss.

When the Mind Leads the Body Follows

"If you want to change the way you look,
then change the way you think."

Change Your Mind—Change Your Body

There are a few things in life that are simply impossible to alter or change. The past, for instance. And yes, you can probably think of a few other things in your life that may appear just as difficult or challenging as trying to change what happened yesterday.

Losing weight may be at the top of your list of things considered tough to change. Certainly, trying to change your body weight or image without first changing your mind would be next to impossible to do. Unfortunately many people try to do just that—change their body without first changing their mindset.

Sure, it's exciting to attempt difficult things, but why make any challenge more difficult than it has to be? Feeling empty-handed and a day older at the end of the day isn't much fun or very rewarding.

So, keep things simple.

If you want to change the way your body looks, then you first have to change the way you think.

Here's the simple truth.

When the mind leads, the body follows.

Let's be honest, exercising is not an innate human reflex. In fact, many people would rather do anything besides exercising their body. It's going to take a little mental effort to get the body moving before any routine becomes a healthy habit.

The easiest and simplest way to change your mindset is to first realize that just starting is the toughest thing to do.

The wonderful news, however, is that any beginning is nothing more than a fleeting moment lasting mere seconds. The very moment you blast past the imaginary "wall" that you have constructed in your mind, your body also will begin moving in the same direction.

So, change the way you look, change your mind.

Use It or Lose It

Some truisms are as old as the hills. One of my favorite adages happens to be, "Use it or lose it."

Incidentally, we're not talking about your money.

We're talking about your body.

And your mind.

We have just learned that a healthy body follows a healthy mind. But, I also would like to emphasize that a healthy mind follows a healthy body.

Since the mind and body are truly inseparable from each other, when you're doing something good for one part of the body, the other parts of your body benefit as well.

So, if your body doesn't want to move or change positions, wake things up by energizing your mind with uplifting thoughts. When your mind is enthusiastic, your body will follow.

It's certainly easy to appreciate that when your body feels invigorated and revitalized, your mind also feels rejuvenated and refreshed.

And vice versa.

Perhaps, rather than saying, "use it or lose it," we should say, "use them both or eventually lose them both."

Who knows, subscribing to this ideology may help you feel twice as fit, especially, if by any chance, you've been remiss about using part of your body.

So, stay balanced and "use them or lose them."

Think Yourself Thin

Have you ever been emotionally in a state of mind that caused you to overeat or eat something you knew you shouldn't consume?

Sure! We all have.

Aside from eating food for all the well-known health reasons, sometimes people will eat solely for the purpose of seeking pleasure and looking for immediate gratification. Other times, people will eat food to temporarily mask or disguise unpleasant feelings or thoughts that they are experiencing. Regardless of the reasons as to why you eat, what you eat can be a powerful tool to change your frame of mind.

Let's look at the other side of the coin.

Can the thoughts that you put in your brain not only change your attitude, but also your health and body weight?

Absolutely.

We have all heard the phrase, "Be careful, you're going to worry or think yourself sick." Surely, if thoughts are powerful enough to make someone ill or troubled, they are undoubtedly strong enough to affect the things people eat or don't eat.

If you believe that you can think yourself into a mindset that causes you to overeat, then you also can think yourself into a state of mind that causes you to eat less.

Remember, there are generally two sides to your thoughts: the positive side and the negative side.

The potential outcomes between these two ways of thinking are virtually immeasurable.

So, is it possible to think yourself thin? Absolutely.

Feed your brain with uplifting thoughts. The first thoughts that come to my mind are:

Think that you can be thinner.

Know that you will be thinner.

Then enjoy all the wonderful health and fitness benefits of being thinner.

Chin Up

It is our attitude at the beginning of a difficult undertaking which, more than anything else, will determine its successful outcome.

— William James, 1842-1910

Stretch Your Mind Before Exercising Your Body

Are you annoyed by those stubborn pounds that won't go away?

Here's a tip.

Start *stretching* your mind before you even think about exercising your body.

Visualization, or what I call "stretching your mind," is nothing new. People have been doing it for years, perhaps without knowing its immeasurable influence on their lives. Thoughts, daydreams, fantasies, and impressions are examples of the visualization process.

Visualization means power.

Although it cannot perform miracles or instantly make you thin, visualization remains one of the best ways to gain insight and find solutions to challenges.

When you are "stretching your mind" you are actually using imagery as a tour guide helping you find clear directions in your journeys. As a powerful vehicle for change, visualization can help you achieve goals, improve self-esteem, overcome fears, and get you unblocked and ready to move and exercise your body.

Since unstretched minds lying dormant over time tend to cause bodies to squeak, creak, and collect fat, you'll need to immediately start stretching.

Your first exercise is to see yourself as a visionary where nothing is impossible. Take your time, this could make you a little sore.

Did you do it?

Good.

Here are a few more brain stretches you can work on this week.

See yourself trimmer.

See yourself fitter.

See yourself eating more healthy foods.

See yourself moving more.

See yourself in new clothes—that actually fit.

Yes, as a dreamer, you have the freedom and power to stretch your mind to the point that the shape of your body will eventually mirror the boundary of your thoughts.

According to Carl Sanburg, "Nothing happens unless first a dream."

So true.

So, start dreaming more.

Start *stretching* more.

In no time your mind will be warmed up and ready for the next step: warming up your muscles. And with a little time, your focus will be on your shape and condition, not on your weight. Just simply shifting your attention from a problem to a solution greatly increases your chance of making a big difference.

The weight issue will take care of itself as you become more physically fit. Transferring the weight from your waist, chin, and buttocks to your biceps, shoulders, and back gives you a tapered and fit look that will help destroy those unwelcome fat silos.

Stay focused.

Ignore the pounds.

They'll eventually get the cold shoulder and go away.

The Problem is Part of the Answer

Are you interested in finding answers to why you're facing challenges to managing your weight?

I thought so.

Interestingly, answers to questions usually follow in the questions's own wake. In other words, ask important or critical questions and you will get intelligent and insightful answers. For instance, ask yourself "What can I specifically eat or not eat, do or not do, to alter my diet and level of activity," rather than simply asking, "Why am I overweight?"

Do you hear the subtle, but important difference between the two questions? The first question is empowering. In essence, the question encourages you to find answers and solutions to specific challenges or problems.

Since the second question, "Why am I overweight?" falls flat, it asks for nothing more than a simple answer. If you're interested in the answer, here it is. People are overweight because they are either eating more calories than they're burning or they're burning less calories than they need to eat.

Period.

So, back to the first, much more important question, "What are you eating or not eating, doing or not doing to affect your weight?"

What is causing you to have a caloric imbalance?

Identifying the cause may help you solve the mystery.

Sound simple?

Good.

Let's do a little self-reflection.

Thinking about why, when, and where we eat, are generally not topics that people are thrilled about. Knowing what triggers or provokes episodes of eating or gorging, however, can be quite helpful in identifying motives that cause you to overeat or consume specific foods in your diet.

On the next page is a short list of possible factors that may influence your eating habits. With a small check mark, identify any factors below that you think may potentially affect your eating habits. Please note that the factors in the table below are not listed in any particular order of ranking or importance.

Hopefully by doing this simple exercise, you will be able to identify and better appreciate various factors that may be influencing your dietary habits.

Hormones	Taste
Stress	Texture
Worry	Odor
Frustration	Flavor
Boredom	Appearance
Low self-esteem	Temperature
Ignorance	Palatability
Destructive habits	Freshness
Disappointments	Packaging
Unfulfilled needs	Cost of food
Depression	Inadequate planning
Climate	Misconceptions
Seasonal changes	Appetite
Temperature	Hunger
Time of day	Physical activities
Availability of food	Injuries
Advertisements	Certain diseases
Convenience	Disabilities
Television	Inactivity
Customs	Illness
Beliefs	Aging
Attitudes	Sleep patterns
Peer influences	Stomach distension
Holiday gatherings	Medications
Cultural practices	Alcohol and drugs
Recreational activities	Tobacco (nicotine)

Break Cycles—Not Records

Losing weight is not about setting records.

It's about breaking cycles or unproductive behavioral habits that repeat themselves.

Off-and-on dieting or *cycling*, as it is sometimes called, usually ends up doing no more than breaking your will and patience to win.

Try leaving setting record time trials to trained athletes.

Focus instead on breaking certain cycles or habits that are key to successfully losing weight. Remember, a habit is an acquired behavioral pattern developed and nurtured by repetition.

Habits feed on repetition.

Habits can be big or small.

Healthy or unhealthy.

But, here's the good news.

Just as habits are learned, they can be unlearned. Good habits are managed by reinforcing healthy habits and weeding out those that are unhealthy or unproductive.

Unlearning begins with a single conscious thought that a particular action brings more pain than pleasure. For instance, up until now, your resulting weight gain has been most likely associated with more long-term pain than with the short-term pleasure you experienced from eating certain things that caused your weight gain.

To change any habit, your thinking must include a conscious decision or commitment to substitute an old behavior with a new one.

Give it a try.

It's exciting.

In no time you may be breaking both cycles and records.

Follow Your Thoughts—Not Wandering Footprints

Habit rules the unreflecting herd.

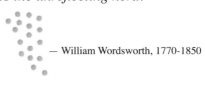

— William Wordsworth, 1770-1850

Habits Make Us—After We Make Them

The Greek philosopher Aristotle, two thousand years ago, wrote, "We are what we repeatedly do." Today his message is still as prophetic as when the words were first written.

Aristotle's brilliant observation that, we become what we repeatedly do, strongly supports the notion that habits feed on repetition.

Now, let's apply Aristotle's message to your eating habits. It reads like this, "You are what you repeatedly EAT."

Does the message hit close to home?

I thought so.

Plain and simple, your weight and physical well-being are forged by your habits. Unfortunately, any of those late night "feeding frenzies" could potentially blossom into a concern if you start learning that gorging fulfills or satisfies a certain need. When your mind makes the connection between intense pleasure and eating unhealthy food, then unhealthy dietary habits emerge.

Here's the great news.

Unlearning an unwanted food habit begins with a single conscious thought that overeating or eating the wrong foods, brings more pain than pleasure into your life.

Next comes a little work.

You may need to remind yourself of this "new discovery" again and again until the message actually seeps deep into your consciousness.

Extinguishing any habit requires reinforcement, repetition, and time, much like the process that formed the habit. Start making more habits that make you who you want to be.

Hidden Treasures

*Appreciation is a wonderful thing: It makes
what is excellent in others belong to us as well.*

— Voltaire, 1694-1778

Appreciation Days

One of the simplest rules in psychology states that people usually take care of the things they appreciate and value, and ignore or mistreat the things that are of little or no value to them.

For instance, would anyone buy an expensive car and then start neglecting it by replacing the motor oil with dirty motor oil?

I hope not.

Is it even thinkable that anyone would take meticulous care of their possessions, yet neglect to take care of their most prized possessions—their inner self and their own physical body?

Astonishingly and unfortunately, yes.

A strong favorable self-image is one of the most treasured and coveted attributes anyone can possess. Feelings of strength, confidence, courage, and peace flourish for those who choose to appreciate and take care of themselves.

A person's self-esteem is not permanently etched in stone. It's constantly reshaped and molded with each new experience. Every day, conscious and unconscious signals are sent to your brain to evaluate your self-worth. In that process, you either choose to foster positive feelings or hang on to negative thoughts.

Each day choosing uplifting thoughts that gently remind you how unique and special you are is critical to your self-image. This touchy-feely stuff is not about being self-centered, it's about getting centered and balanced.

Now.

Get out a pen and your calendar.

Start marking the days, weeks, and months of your calendar with words of appreciation. Be bold, call them "Gratefulness Days." You should have a full calendar when you're done writing.

On those special "appreciation" days, and the days between them, constantly remind yourself again and again of how special you are.

Is it possible to start changing your self-image and weight by simply appreciating yourself a little bit more?

Absolutely.

The Weight of Words

Words are fascinating.

The actual physical weight of spoken words cannot be measured or weighed, yet they have the potential to carry considerable weight and lasting impact on our behavior when they're used.

We use them in many different ways to communicate and share thoughts and ideas with each other.

That's not new.

But, it may be interesting to note that words often are used to communicate with ourself. It's much like having a quiet conversation with no one around—in essence, you're talking to yourself.

Be careful of the little chatty discussions you have with yourself. Imagine the results if you were to say to yourself, "I can't lose weight," or "I love to eat."

People who tell themselves that they love to eat, do just that, they eat and eat. The people who tell themselves that they can't manage their weight find it almost unbearable to put the fork or spoon down.

Just listen to the contrast between the different messages that are being sent to the center of a person's brain.

I can't control my desire to eat or snack. (Weak)

I can control my eating habits. (Strong)

I will control my eating habits! (Strongest)

I've always been out of shape. (So)

I'm thinking about getting in shape. (Good)

I will get in better shape! (Fantastic)

It will take me forever to change. (Stop, don't say that)

I will change someday. (Marginal)

I will succeed and nothing will stop me! (Phenomenal)

I'm working tirelessly to change the past. (Good luck)

The future is more important than the past. (I agree)

I'll learn from the past, I'll anticipate the future, but I'll live in the present! (Bingo)

Your future is determined by what you say and do today. Your weight tomorrow will be determined by exactly what you eat and do right now, at this very moment.

There is no other way.

Nagging Makes Me Hungry

Most people love to eat.

And eat.

And eat.

And eat.

And should an ordinary meal ever turn into a self-inflicted *banquet* or food jamboree, our loved ones are usually standing nearby, ready to offer an assortment of advice, opinions, and counsel.

To mute the barrage of badgering advice or annoying notes left solely for your own personal gain, you habitually return to the refrigerator to hunt for some comfort or solace.

Yes, there are many reasons why people overeat.

Anxiety being a common cause.

Nagging another.

Stress, too.

The list is long!

Regardless of the reason, it seems there's no shortage of excuses that can be employed by any of us to justify a food jubilee, especially when the pursuit is on for something tasty to devour.

Since food elicits great pleasure and reduces tension and can temporarily stave off stress, one must look for alternatives to the nagging approach to change behaviors.

Here's an idea.

Try posting positive affirmations on your desk, stove, refrigerator, or bathroom mirror. Wherever, it doesn't matter. They just need to be seen. Just stick an affirmation on it.

Affirmations are positive phrases or images rehearsed again and again in your mind. Making affirmations is a way of gently preparing your mind to accept new ways of thinking.

There is nothing more inspiring than affirmations that abound with enthusiasm and optimism.

Sometimes it takes only a little hope to change your

attitude or perspective. That smidgen of faith may be found in as little as two words: I can. Or even one word: yes.

Affirmations are not cure-alls, but they do offer a way to send uplifting messages directly to your brain. So, the next time you're tempted to look for an excuse to snack, look for an affirmation instead.

Entice yourself.

You'll be miles ahead and calories behind.

Know Excuses

It's easy to find a reason or justification for almost anything. Tossing reason to the wind is not an uncommon practice, especially when someone is bent on indulging their taste buds or appetite.

I love these explanations for overeating.

"It's Friday night."

"Just this once."

"Let's celebrate."

"I won't do it again."

"I need something to cheer me up."

"We bought it, we can't throw it away."

Sound familiar?

Maybe too familiar?

Don't be too hard on yourself. We all make excuses now and then. It's quite normal.

What is important, however, is that you realize that you're making excuses. Only when you understand and KNOW that you're making excuses, can you say NO to your excuses.

So, the next time you try justifying the need to devour a bag of chips because you THINK you might be deficient in salt, you'll know you're just making excuses.

Know excuses.

No excuses.

No regrets.

Ninety-nine percent of failures come from people who have the habit of making excuses.

— George Washington Carver, 1864-1943

Nudge Me—Don't Shove Me

Let's be honest. Most of us need a little "pinch" now and then to get inspired to follow through on things we would love to accomplish.

Right?

Okay.

Motivation is a "tug and nudge" phenomenon. All of us, at one time or another, are pushed and pulled by our basic desires and needs: food, health, security, and love being the most fundamental needs. Similarly, we are pulled along by incentives and rewards—success and money being powerful motivators.

For us to stay motivated or inspired we need to be constantly tugged and nudged. It's that simple.

We can initially be driven to desire something, but without an incentive, motivation eventually evaporates and disappears. Motivation, by its very nature, has many interesting facets. A person, for example, who overeats to satisfy a ravenous appetite for food is highly motivated by the pleasures that delicious foods provide. Similarly, distress can be a powerful motivator prompting people to seek comfort in overeating. In contrast, the distress or discomfort associated with being physically unfit and overweight may be the motivating factors that drive some people to make personal changes in their lifestyle.

Regardless of the motivational factors required to alter a person's behavior, the driving force for change is found in one's need to avoid pain and suffering and seek pleasure and rewards.

Remember, being shoved or tackled isn't very amusing or pleasurable to anyone who's trying their best to find their way in life.

Love me.

Nudge me.

There's no need to shove me.

Wait Reduction

Are you seriously interested in losing weight?

The first step toward any successful weight loss must start with putting an end to the "waiting game," or what I'll call the "someday" syndrome.

"Someday I'll lose weight."

Sound familiar?

Too familiar?

Incidentally, *someday* exists for people who avoid doing things they believe they won't or can't do now.

Actually, there is nothing easier, for any of us, than putting off until tomorrow the things that need to be done today.

Waiting for the perfect time or just the right moment to start losing weight is usually a complete waste of your time.

"Someday," "maybe tomorrow," "but not today," just won't work for you any longer.

It surely hasn't ever worked for anyone else.

So.

Begin losing unwanted pounds today by using one of your biggest weapons against stubborn weight.

The weapon is actually nothing more than acquiring a philosophy that encourages WAIT REDUCTION.

Here is how simple the concept is to use.

First, don't be a "Wait Watcher." Earning this title is only accomplished by waiting and watching the days, weeks, and years slip by.

Not smart.

Remember, good "Wait Watchers" are lousy dieters.

For quicker results, start your diet today.

Lose your *wait* control.

Here's to losing weight.

Remember, ALWAYS consult with your physician before starting any diet or exercise program.

Radiate With Enthusiasm

Let your enthusiasm radiate in your voice, your actions, your facial expressions, your personality, the words you use, and the thoughts you think! Nothing great was ever achieved without enthusiasm.

— Ralph Waldo Emerson, 1803-1882

Sunny Side Up

Let's be daringly simplistic.

There are three kinds of people.

People who are positive most of the time.

People who are negative most of the time.

And people who find themselves somewhere in the middle between being pessimistic and optimistic.

May I dare ask the question, what possible benefit or advantage is there to viewing life from a dismal or gloomy point of view?

None!

Everything in this world, including losing weight and getting healthier, is much easier with a positive attitude working for you.

It may sound funny, but confronting life's many challenges has been known to make some people feel like a carton of cooked eggs.

Sometimes boiled.

Sometimes scrambled.

And sometimes grilled or pan fried.

So, the next time you start to feel a bit "cooked" or overwhelmed about losing weight and getting in shape, just think positively. The moment you learn that you can quickly change how you feel by simply focusing your attention on positive thoughts, you then will be instantly in command of your mood, in charge of your feelings, and in control of your diet.

So, stay positive.

Stay sunny side up.

Sweet Treats

*The sweetest pleasure arises
from difficulties overcome.*

 — Publius Syrus, 85-43 B.C

Bells, Buzzers, and Horns

Snap.

Crackle.

Crunch.

I love to hear these sounds.

Listen carefully.

You can hear these sounds inside your head when you grind, nibble, and chew food.

Without the munching and chomping sounds, eating would be less pleasurable and certainly less exciting.

Bite into a mushy overripe spongy apple.

Yuck.

Try biting into a stale cracker or soggy piece of toast.

The result is the same.

Yuck.

Now, bite into a fresh crisp apple.

Snap.

Can you hear the beautiful snapping sound right in the center of your brain?

It's blissful.

You have just been introduced to the concept of "bells, buzzers, and horns." In biology, they're called cell receptors. These microscopic sensors not only allow us to smell and taste things, but they, along with three other cell sensors, allow us to perceive the world around us.

Amazingly, your appetite or interest in eating food is impacted by all five of your senses.

Sight, touch, taste, smell, and hearing.

It's no wonder we love to eat.

And eat. And eat.

Your tongue and brain sensor cells can easily fall in love with the attention they get when your palate embraces a delightful bite of your favorite creamy, crunchy, nutty dessert.

Have any doubts?

Then give it a try.

You'll notice with each watery mouthful of various blends of exotic flavors, accented with small crunchy chewy surprises, that you will unconsciously start hearing the most beautiful horns, trumpets, wispy violins, and ever-so-sweet oboes sounding off silently in your mind.

Ring.

Ding.

Toot.

Toot.

Many people, unsatisfied with just *music*, enhance their dining experiences with *firework* displays. Depending on their mood, and time of the day, their brain receptors are either showered with caffeine, doused with alcohol, or smothered with nicotine-laden smoke.

Buzz.

Buzz.

And on goes the cycle of enchantment as it repeats itself again and again throughout one's life. Each day begins and ends alike. Dietary habits are coaxed, molded, and forged by pleasure seeking receptors that are waiting patiently to be stimulated.

One pound after another pound.

Stop it! End this cycle now!

May I make a suggestion?

Turn down the volume inside your head. Over stimulation or amplification can be deadening—quite literally.

I'm not suggesting that you start eating cold, soggy, and tasteless food to quiet your taste receptors. I'm suggesting that you enjoy the natural taste of food without adding spices and ingredients that send your tongue and brain sensors into orbit.

Now it just may be the right time for your brain to develop an appetite for quieter *music*.

Try listening to a string quartet or a peaceful sonata.

Here's to resting your taste buds and listening to your good old senses.

Keep Your Eyes Off It and Your Nose Out of It

Don't look at *it*.
Don't smell *it*.
Don't touch *it*.
And don't even think about buying *it*.
Walk right on past *it*.
And don't look back.

Sight, smell, and taste are three of the strongest factors that can arouse your appetite. Appetite is your mind's desire or interest in eating certain foods, regardless of whether you're hungry. The temptation or passion to eat can be so intense with people having BIG appetites that even after their hunger or the physiological need for food has been satisfied, their interest in eating feverishly continues.

Keep your appetite under control.

Don't even think about tempting your senses with a brief encounter with an unguarded, ready to eat, old-fashioned oven baked crispy apple or peach pie. The mere inkling of seeing the golden brown crust of any pie can send some people's appetite into orbit.

Keep your nose in the air, your eyes in your head, and your hands in your pockets.

Food that's out of sight is out of mind.

Good luck keeping your senses in check and your appetite in control.

No Show

Are you looking for new ways to "watch what you eat"? Look no farther.

One of the best ways to "watch what you eat," is to "not look at what you eat."

It's that simple.

Just looking at food can make you hungry.

Staring at large bowls of delicious food twelve inches from your eyes won't help you lose weight.

So, clear your dinner table of all serving dishes. Extra helpings of food either belong in your refrigerator or on top of your kitchen stove. Completely away from sight.

"No Show" means, "Don't Show."

Here's a little suggestion.

Be a "no show," and don't appeal to your appetite.

With this advice, you won't have to *watch* what you eat— it will be out of sight and out of your reach!

Mood Food

Can different kinds of foods influence your mental disposition or state of mind?

Absolutely.

Certain foods can have an incredibly strong impact on changing your mood. Understanding the biology and chemistry of foods and how they affect human behavior, however, can be an overwhelmingly complex issue. This book is simply not the place to unravel the mystery and science of chemical compounds that affect mood changes and food intake.

However, all of us can recognize the subtle mood changes after biting into a favorite dessert, sipping a coveted beverage, or munching on a tantalizing snack.

The results are immediate.

Mood changes are usually first detected in a person's face. Facial transformations can vary from a silly grin to a little smirk. Regardless of facial expressions, mood swings usually become more and more ecstatic with each helping of their favorite foods.

More helpings.

More bliss.

Not all foods, however, will elicit these enchanting moments.

Celery won't.

Nor will white rice or bland cereal mush.

I'm sure you know very well which foods will or won't produce a smile.

If you're using food to change your mood, you may want to take a small step back and reconsider your approach to eating. Remember, food was never meant to be a substitute for friendships, accomplishments, vacations, love, or security.

Quite frankly, devouring a half gallon of ice cream in the evening is a poor substitute for taking the dog for a walk.

Start now.

Stop confusing food with mood.
Feed your body food.
Feed you soul experiences.
In no time you'll be changing your mood without food.
Good luck.
And have fun.

I Don't Love You Anymore

Love always prevails.

I'm a romantic at heart, but as the old saying goes, "It takes two to tango."

Relationships of all types have the potential to change and morph into different unions and partnerships.

Some relationships seem to have been blessed and then forged to create a bond strong enough to last an entire lifetime. These loving bonds are robust enough to brave any storm, and supple enough to weather some of the most fickle times.

On the other hand, there are other relationships that appear to culminate and end about as fast as they begin. Their union, although initially close, was simply not strong enough from the beginning to hold the relationship together.

We can learn much from short-lived relationships, especially when the *love affair* from the start was with food and not with another person.

Be honest.

How many times have you heard someone say, "I love ice cream," or simply, "I love eating."

Trust me, these people are in love.

But, it's a transitory love!

As soon as their eyes are taken off their luscious snacks and the food is devoured, swallowed, and on its way to their waistline, the brief love affair crumbles as the words, "I don't love you anymore" become all too evident and painful.

So, be stern.

Be selective.

And be especially careful of all relationships with things that may wind up hanging on or clinging to you. If need be, divorce yourself from foods or snacks that want nothing more than to be married to your thighs.

You Are What You Eat

What we love, we shall grow to resemble.

— Bernard of Clairvaux, 1090-1153

Garbage In—Garbage In

On the surface, it seems ridiculous to think that some people, at various times of their life, subconsciously use their bodies as *Dumpsters* or trash bins. Have you ever unwittingly assumed this role by scavenging or *inhaling* "junk food," while comfortably slouched on a couch mesmerized by a television set, with your TV remote in hand?

No, I didn't think so.

Well anyway, click, click, click is a common sound in front of a television set. And so is, munch, munch, munch.

The nutritional quality of the food eaten by some folks is, quite frankly, incompatible with sustaining or promoting good health.

When people eat junk food, the *trash* gradually collects inside their bodies. This concept may help explain why illnesses such as heart disease, obesity, diabetes, hypertension, and various forms of cancer, just to mention a few, are associated directly with the amount of *garbage* in one's diet.

Remember, garbage in doesn't equal garbage out.

Sorry!

Garbage in equals garbage in.

So get healthy.

Take out the *trash*.

Eat well.

Don't Run Out of Gas on a Full Tank

Do you get tired too easily?

If you have ever felt like you're "out of gas," or your body is "running on empty," even after *tanking* up on a huge meal, you're not alone.

You have company.

Many people are eager to jump-start their busy days by loading up on high *octane* drinks and sugary snacks. Regardless of how much they put in their *tank*, the kick they feel from the extra shots of sugar and caffeine is short-lived.

So, the next time you stop to fill up, be careful of pumping drinks and snacks into your body that can cause an initial blood sugar spike, followed by the dreaded blood sugar plunge.

Do your body good.

Keep your energy level sustained by eating only wholesome nutritionally packed foods. Oh, and don't forget to keep your *radiator* full of fresh water. Overheating and easy physical exhaustion are symptoms of low body fluids.

It's just not smart to run out of gas on a full tank.

So remember, select only high grade fuels for your body.

And always keep a check on your water level.

Drink plenty of fresh, clean water.

Get Some Therapy

There are many kinds of therapies that people seek to help them solve their challenges. Some therapies can be quite expensive, very involved, and not necessarily designed or applicable for all ages.

No one, however, is too young or too old to benefit from some old-fashioned replacement *therapy*.

Prescriptions and medications, well, let's leave that to the medical doctors to prescribe.

Ready for a little *therapy*?

Let's begin.

Start your replacement *therapy* today by substituting the processed foods in your diet with more fresh foods. You know the foods I'm talking about.

This small but very important change to your diet will give you not only momentum but plenty of time throughout the next few days to make a list of foods that should be added or removed from your diet.

Here's a few suggestions to get you started.

Use herbs and spices instead of salt to flavor your food.

Enjoy Sundays instead of sundaes.

And think about the health benefit of hitting more tennis balls and eating fewer meatballs.

My favorite replacement *therapy* is saying "CHEESE" instead of eating cheese. It's not only the best way to have your picture taken, it's also a great way to reduce your fat consumption.

Decreasing your intake of calories, cholesterol, saturated fats, salt, butter, cheese, meats, sour cream, processed foods, cream-based sauces, artificial flavors and dyes, sugars, and low-fiber foods, is just good old-fashioned therapy.

Now that's good *medicine* worth swallowing.

Think Differently—Eat Differently

*"Eating healthy foods should put your mind at ease,
eating unhealthy foods should unsettle your nerves."*

Comfort Foods

Have you ever felt the need to seek consolation or solace from eating your favorite *comfort* foods?

I thought so.

Now, more than ever, many people currently are sick or will at some time in their life become quite ill simply from eating the wrong foods.

Obesity, heart disease, diabetes, and cancer are only a few of the major diseases associated with poor dietary habits.

Now, for the good news.

Generally, it's never too late in life to start improving your diet and refining your lifestyle choices so that you can reduce the probability of suffering from some debilitating disease.

That is precisely why it's so critical to emphasize the importance of including more *comfort* foods in your diet. Since there's a huge list of *comfort* foods to choose from, you must be careful in your selection.

The real purpose or intent behind eating *comfort* foods is to put your mind at ease, not to try to calm your nerves. Knowing that you're doing everything in your power to reduce the risk of a potentially life-threatening ailment by eating only the very best fresh foods should be quite consoling.

Quite frankly, how could anyone be relieved, reassured, or comforted by eating foods that are known to cause serious health problems?

Not me.

Disease promoting foods are not *comfort* foods, they're high-anxiety foods.

Period.

So, rethink your definition of *comfort* foods

In very little time, you will begin to appreciate that only the highest quality wholesome foods earn the "*comfort* food" seal of approval.

With this new interpretation of the meaning of *comfort*

foods, you'll completely appreciate why health enthusiasts don't find any solace from eating unhealthy, processed foods loaded with sugar, salt, fat, and calories.

So, comfort your mind.

Reassure yourself, and eat well.

Get Fresh

Here's an interesting fact.

All the foods we eat were once alive.

Granted, this is not a common thought to entertain before eating a meal, but it's worth noting that the ingredients of a tuna or turkey sandwich, or for that matter, a tossed green salad, were once living things.

Yes, as ridiculous as it may sound, even a french fry was once alive as a simple potato before it was ripped from the ground and processed with oil and salt.

Seriously.

Think about it.

All foods have two lives. The "before" and the "thereafter" life. In farm language, we're talking about pre- and post-harvest times.

Let's be frank.

The shelf life of foods is relatively short without the addition of chemical preservatives to artificially prolong their existence.

Applying this novel way of thinking about fresh, whole foods, you can see that fresh foods have very short "thereafter" lives.

Why not increase the odds of prolonging and enhancing the quality of your life by eating more fresh, whole foods that didn't have their *lives* prolonged with chemical additives?

Make smart decisions.

Get the best whenever you can.

Get fresh as often as you can.

Get Real

Who knows when, where, and why the expression "get real" originated in the lexicon of words and phrases. I'm not even sure what the actual phrase means or what the implications are for its use. But, I do know that using the idiom "get real" can be a very useful reminder to eat wholesome, nutritious foods at every opportunity given to us.

In an age when many people are eating foods that are either refined, processed, treated, or artificially manufactured, it just may be worth taking a few moments to think about the quality of foods you're putting into your body.

The less processed a food is, the more whole or wholesome the food is.

It's that simple.

So, the next time you go grocery shopping, apply a new meaning to the jargon "get real." And let this shopping tip encourage you to buy real or whole foods.

Get real.

Get healthy.

Meals—Not Pills

First things first.

There's no substitute for preparing healthy meals and eating nutritious snacks.

Are there times, however, when nutritional supplements are not only potentially valuable but also recommended by professionals in the health and medical fields?

Certainly.

Are there times when it's a better idea to indiscriminately pop nutritional supplements instead of preparing and eating healthy meals and snacks?

Certainly not.

Health and weight concerns can become a problem when an individual develops a false sense of protection or assurance from popping mega doses of dietary supplements during an "eat whatever—eat whenever" phase of their life.

Don't misuse or misconstrue the intended meaning of the slogan "meals—not pills." In the context of this book, "meals—not pills" is a catchphrase used ONLY to gently remind us of the importance of eating healthy meals instead of indiscriminately using nutritional supplements to compensate for eating poorly.

Remember, always consult with your physician if you have any concerns or questions about your diet or any supplements that you may be taking or considering using.

Use Your Mind To See

Knowledge is the true organ of sight, not eyes.

— Panchatantra, 5th Century A.D.

Open Your Eyes Before You Open Your Mouth

First things first.

Before you open your mouth—it's a good idea to first open your eyes. In other words, know what you're eating before you eat it.

The easiest way to learn about what you're eating is by reading food labels. Food labels can serve you well. They can act as useful "food selection filters" to quickly inform you of the nutritional contents before you even think about purchasing the package of food.

Packaged food products labeled with funny names or sold in packages printed with colorful monsters on the cover should be one of your first clues or warning signs that the manufacturer may be trying to appeal to your fascination with processed foods that are often loaded with sugar, salt, and fat, rather than to your need for fresh foods.

You'll be much better off and more informed if you read the nutritional label as well as the subtle messages hidden between the lines.

Unprocessed natural whole foods, on the other hand, usually don't have foods labels, fancy names, and other intentionally added things to prolong their shelf life. Isn't it interesting just how much nutritional information we can glean from looking at the shell or skin of fresh, natural whole foods that don't have labels divulging huge volumes of information about themselves? Just looking at the red skin of a freshly grown tomato tells me that it's healthier to eat the tomato than to eat a can of processed tomato soup.

Are you ready to test your knowledge?

Good.

Which food is healthier—potatoes or potato chips?

Apples or apple pie?

Carrots or carrot cake?

The quiz is over.

I'm sure you did just fine.

The sugar, salt, fat, and caloric differences between these foods is staggering.

Your assignment—before you even think about opening a can or box—is to first open your eyes.

Start *reading* labels.

You'll be amazed how much you will understand about the importance of eating more nutritious whole foods that may or may not come canned or boxed with printed labels.

Fast Foods Are Naturally the Best

Let's have an eating contest!

Who do you think is going to eat first? The person who peels a banana? Or the person who drives their car or truck up to a drive-up fast food window?

You may be pleasantly surprised by the results.

Foods that are baked, deep-fried, grilled, broiled, or processed require much more time to prepare than healthy *fast foods* that are simply handled or washed before they're eaten.

Still not convinced?

Consider the time difference between baking a cake or pie and making a fruit salad. You'll be finished eating your fruit salad long before the pie or cake is ready to serve.

If you slow down, reevaluate, and identify the *fast foods* you've been missing while at the drive-up windows, you'll have more time to stock your kitchen with nutritious *fast foods*.

Good nutrition begins with eating nutritious foods to promote and sustain health. We have a tendency to live longer when we eat to live, rather than live to eat.

The choices and decisions you make daily about what types of food to eat have a tremendous impact on your health and vitality. Food is much more than a source of energy; eating a variety of nutritious foods gives us the essential nutrients we need on a regular basis.

Essential nutrients must be obtained from our diet, since the body doesn't manufacture them. The six nutrient groups are carbohydrates (sugars and starches), lipids (fats), proteins, vitamins, minerals, and water.

Carbohydrate, fat, and protein are the three fuel nutrients burned by the body to provide energy. Alcohol is a rich source of energy, but it is considered a toxic nutrient and has no place among the essential nutrients.

Although we obtain zero energy from vitamins, minerals,

and water, certain vitamins and minerals act like spark plugs, setting energy-yielding nutrients on fire.

Vitamins and minerals do much more than burn fuels. As organic nutrients, vitamins also are required in very small quantities in the diet to perform many vital functions that include reproduction, vision, bone development, and blood formation and clotting.

Minerals are special types of inorganic nutrients that also are required in very small quantities for the purpose of serving the needs of billions of body cells. Some of the major functions include growth and repair of body tissues, transmission of nerve impulses, regulation of muscle contraction, maintenance of water balance, and structural roles.

Water is an important lubricant. It works to cool and maintain normal cell operation. In fact, every single living cell in your body requires water to function properly.

Good nutrition leads to good living.

Next time you want to win a race.

Eat *fast foods*!

An Enlightening Lesson From a Little Calorie

Concerned about those pesky calories in the foods you love to eat? There's certainly good reason to be!

A calorie is a unit of energy so small that it takes about 3,500 calories to equal one pound of body fat. Often called a kilocalorie (kcal), the calorie is the easiest way for us to relate to the energy value of different foods and drinks.

Could a few extra calories a day, day in and day out, be the reason why three out of four people in the United States are overweight or obese?

Absolutely.

Here is where the smallest things can make the biggest difference.

Amazing as it may seem, eating just one extra mouthful of food each day for a year can explain the two or so pounds of weight gain on the hips, butts, thighs, and stomachs of many unsuspecting people throughout that same year.

Imagine the results with eating two or three mouthfuls of extra food each day for several years.

About fifteen pounds.

So, here's the good news.

Consuming just 150 fewer calories a day, the equivalent of drinking one 12-ounce soda, may not seem like a significant change to your diet, but it's enough to cause your body to lose about 15 pounds of fat a year, all other things being equal.

That's great news for not having to make huge lifestyle changes. Remember, it's the *little* things that you eat or don't eat on a regular basis that make the biggest difference in your weight.

So, why not give up a few calories and teach those little guys a big lesson.

Empty Calories Aren't Very Empty

Two concepts will help explain and simplify the enormously complex field of nutrition science as it relates to helping people balance their diets.

Variety.

And nutritional density.

Notwithstanding any special health or medical concerns, as a general rule, eating a mixture of diverse, fresh whole foods from different food groups that are naturally rich in nutrients and lower in calories, is one of the single most important and easiest things you can do to improve your diet.

Nutritionally dense healthy foods, by definition, have a high nutrient-to-calorie ratio. This simply means that the foods are providing plenty of nutrients without subjecting you to too many calories.

Less healthy foods have a significantly lower nutrient-to-calorie ratio. Basically, low nutritionally dense foods are high in calories and lower in nutrients. Eating more unhealthy foods crammed with sugar and fat translates into eating less healthy foods missing important essential nutrients that your body needs.

Anyone who is trying to maintain or lose weight and is eating "empty calorie" foods that are high in sugar and fat, will be forced to cut back on nutritious foods.

Not a good idea.

Remember, empty calories aren't very empty.

They're jammed, packed, and stuffed with everything but nutrients.

Hold the Mayo—Please!

Sometimes it's the little things you eat or don't eat that make the biggest difference in determining your success in losing weight. It's interesting to note that most people who are overweight usually don't eat all that much extra food.

The explanation is simple.

A person only has to eat a little extra food each day for an extended period of time in order to gain substantial weight.

Smearing just one slice of plain toast or bread with a dab of butter, margarine, or mayonnaise quickly can add many calories to your diet and extra pounds to your waist. Fatty spreads used only a few times a day will typically add an extra 100 to 200 calories to your diet each day.

In "weight talk" language, this means an average person using one or two tablespoons of butter or margarine a day could paste between 10 and 20 pounds of fat on their body in a single year so long as the extra fat calories consumed were above and beyond the energy required to maintain that person's energy balance.

Let's do some basic math.

One tablespoon of butter or margarine is packed with 100 calories. Interestingly, just one tablespoon of vegetable oil is crammed with 120 calories.

A dab here.

A pat there.

A innocent smear over there.

And a few bites here and there.

That's all the math we'll need to do.

Remember, it's often the small unsuspecting things we eat that ultimately get plastered all over our bodies.

Get a hold on your diet, hold the mayo!

Calories Don't Negotiate

Calories will never negotiate!

I think we should repeat this mantra at least three times before we're tempted to eat something we don't want to wear.

The concept is simple.

Energy cannot be destroyed. It can only be changed from one form to another form. This sounds like something we would learn in a college physics class.

Anyway.

If you eat it and don't need it, you own it.

And what you own, you will wear.

Incidentally, and contrary to popular myth, hot peppers and grapefruit juice won't help you negotiate with excess calories either.

Garlic won't help either.

Potions and lotions are a waste of time and money as well.

Calories listen to three things.

Motion.

Motion.

And more motion.

Exercise your negotiating power.

Move your body to burn calories.

Does It Walk, Swim, or Fly?

Some of the most important principles of nutrition can be reduced to a few common truths. One fundamental law worth observing is realizing that the things you don't eat can be just as important as the things you do eat.

How true.

Let's use our imagination and learn some very important things about the quality of fats in foods by knowing whether your favorite foods once walked, swam, or flew.

Sound weird?

Good.

Let's begin by referring to fish as *Swimmers*.

Let's call the various land dwelling animals either *Walkers*, *Runners*, or *Roamers*.

Goats and sheep can represent the *Walkers*.

Deer and elk can be the *Runners*.

Cows are a good choice to represent the *Roamers*.

Birds will represent the *Flyers*.

And we'll call plants *Sunbathers* because they love the sun so much.

Ready?

All sun loving plants that spend their lives basking in the sun producing fruits, vegetables, grains, cereals, nuts, seeds, and beans, primarily make healthy fats. These fats are called monounsaturated and polyunsaturated fats.

Sunbathers don't have any means to produce cholesterol, and therefore are void of it. This is great news for anyone who wants to limit their intake of cholesterol.

In contrast, the *Walkers*, *Runners*, *Roamers*, and *Flyers* all contain a higher proportion of the less healthy fats, called saturated fats, than do *Sunbathers*.

Last, but not least, are the *Swimmers*, especially the cold-water types, which contain some of the healthiest fats. These healthy fats are called omega-3 fatty acids. Despite the awkward and long names usually given to omega-3 fatty acids, these special fats are quite healthy for your heart.

To greatly lower your consumption of cholesterol and saturated fats, it's best to include more *Sunbathers,* and significantly fewer *Flyers* and *Land Rovers* in your diet.

Cold-Water Swimmers Are the Healthiest

Burr.

Shiver.

Shiver.

Cold-water swimmers love to spend their entire lives in bone chilling water. Some like the frigid waters off the coast of Alaska, others prefer the climate of Nova Scotia.

Regardless of where they swim, they love cold water.

Once they're born and raised in cold water they never want to leave. With a fishing pole and a little tenacity, however, they can be wrestled right out of the chilly waters.

Some of the best known cold-water swimmers are salmon and halibut. Both fish contain some of the healthiest fats you can get in your diet. These fish are loaded with special fats called omega-3 fatty acids.

Without discussing the chemistry of omega-3 fatty acids, it warrants mentioning that these fats are some of the world's best kinds of fats you could possibly eat for the health of your heart.

Cold-water swimmers might be the healthiest, but it's good to know you don't have to dive into a swimming pool filled with icy water in order to do something wonderful for your heart.

Go ahead, include some cold-water swimmers in your diet on a regular basis.

Sometimes a Minus is a Plus

*"What you don't eat can be
as important as what you do eat."*

Pig Out

Let's talk about eating.

It's a worthy topic to discuss because eating is not only important to the quality of your life, but it also can bring great pleasure to your life.

We eat for a number of reasons.

Health.

Enjoyment.

Survival.

I'm sure you can think of other reasons.

In any event, the need to eat is biologically programmed into every living animal and organism on earth.

Naturally, the urge to eat is strong—food and nourishment are vital to life. For some people, however, their incessant drive to eat can be overwhelming—and quite counterproductive.

How many times have you heard the following cliches mentioned in reference to eating?

"Let's pig out."

Or the all too familiar: "Let's hunker down and pork out."

Understanding the subliminal message in these cliches is important to your health and well-being. For years, the hidden meaning of these messages has fallen on deaf ears.

No longer.

Whether you hear the words, "pig out," or "pork out," the point is the same.

"Keep out," or better yet, "watch out."

Yes, all animal products are the major source of cholesterol and saturated fats in a person's diet, both of which are contributing factors to heart and artery disease. So, if you're one of the growing numbers of people who should reduce their intake of animal fats, you may consider what foods should be in or out of your diet:

Keep the *pig* out, and the fruit, vegetables, and grains in your diet.

The next time you happen to hear "oink—oink," or "moo—moo," you'll be reminded of just how important it is to curb your consumption of animal fats.

You can use the table below to quickly estimate the percentage of total calories supplied by fat in various food items.

100 %	Butter • vegetable oils • margarine mayonnaise • salad oils • shortening
70-80+ %	Cheese • bacon • bologna • avocados • olives peanut butter • sour cream • nuts • beef franks
50-60+ %	Hamburgers • french fries • ice cream medium-fat meat • whole milk • potato chips fried chicken • chocolate bars
30-40+ %	2% low-fat milk • cupcakes • biscuits • cookies salmon • lean meat • dark turkey (w/o skin)
20-30+%	Plain low-fat yogurt • 1% low-fat milk oysters • light turkey (w/o skin)
10-20+%	Most kinds of bread • hamburger buns plain pancakes
5-10+%	Beans • shrimp • lobster • cod • clams most breakfast cereals • English muffins
0-5+%	Fruit • skim milk • sugar • rice • colas • pasta spaghetti • most vegetables • bulgur • popcorn

For additional information on the nutrient content of selected foods, you may find it helpful to browse through the Food Composition Tables published by the USDA.

Bloated Figures

Do numbers always tell the whole truth and nothing but the truth, all the time?

No.

Personally, I believe it's a good idea to be a little skeptical about statistics and numbers, especially when they're used to advertise or promote a product that you're not 100 percent familiar with.

Some simple food labels can even be misleading and confusing to the unwary consumer. For instance, low-fat milk is 98 percent fat free when reported on a weight basis, yet almost 40 percent of the calories in low-fat milk still come from fat!

See the difference? Good.

So, don't be mislead by numbers.

Sometimes the easiest way to cut through the confusion is to pay attention to the percentage of total calories supplied by fat or THE TOTAL GRAMS OF FAT you eat each day. Remember, in any given day an average adult consuming about 2,000 calories should not consume more than 60 grams of fat.

So, the next time you read a food label, listen to a manufacturer make a claim about their food products, or estimate your total fat intake, you might want to take a second glance at how the numbers are being represented or reported.

The following table is a quick reference guide to help you see the relationship between grams of fat consumed and the percentage of fat calories in a diet. The numbers are based on consuming a daily 2,000 calorie diet.

Where's the Fat?

Food	Quantity	Grams
Milk (skim)	1 cup (8 oz.)	Trace
Milk (low-fat 1%)	1 cup (8 oz.)	3
Milk (low-fat 2%)	1 cup (8 oz.)	5
Milk (whole 3.3%)	1 cup (8 oz.)	8
Cheese (cheddar)	1 oz.	9
Cheese (American)	1 oz.	9
Cheese (cottage 2%)	1 cup	4
Sour cream (cultured)	1 tbsp	3
Ice cream (11% fat)	1 cup	14
Potato chips	1 oz.	9-10
Peanut butter	1 tbsp	8
Fruit	any	Trace
Vegetables	most	Few
Garbanzo beans (cooked)	1 cup	4
Kidney beans (canned)	1 cup	<1
Almonds (most nuts)	1 oz.	15
Bread (most kinds)	1 slice	1-2
Breakfast cereals (Total®)	1 cup	1
Rice (white cooked)	1 cup	<1
Spaghetti (plain, cooked)	1 cup	1
Salmon (broiled)	3 oz.	9
Shrimp (boiled)	3 oz.	1
Ground beef (16% fat)	3 oz.	14

For additional information on the nutrient content of selected foods, you may find
it helpful to browse through the Food Composition Tables published by the USDA.

Curb Crude Oils

Not all oils and fats are created equal.

There are some healthy oils.

And then there are the unhealthy ones, which I refer to as *crude* or harmful fats. For the sake of your health, it's best to curb or restrict the unhealthy "fats" in your diet because they contain a higher percentage of the unhealthy saturated fats and trans-fats.

Let's learn more.

All plant or vegetable oils are 100 percent fat. The major differences between vegetable oils are reflected in the kinds of *fatty acids* that make up the oils. Oils that are higher in polyunsaturated and monounsaturated fats are much more healthy than saturated fats. Therefore, the quality of an oil is represented by either a higher ratio of polyunsaturated to saturated fats (P/S ratio) or a higher ratio of polyunsaturated and monounsaturated fats to saturated fats (P-M/S ratio).

Understanding the types of fats found in plants and animals is quite simple. Plant fats have a much higher P/S or P-M/S ratio than animal fats, which have a much lower P/S or P-M/S ratio.

Now, you can stuff all this in your head or just remember that plant oils are much healthier than animal fats.

Period.

There are, however, two exceptions to this rule.

Trans-fats, which certain food companies manufacture by hydrogenating vegetable oils, are exceptionally *crude* and unhealthy fats.

Avoid them.

Read labels. Trans-fats are usually found hiding among the crunchy, crispy, chip-like junk foods.

And don't forget the other exception. Omega-3 fats, which are found primarily in cold-water fish, are wonderful fats because of their healthful heart properties.

One last point.

It's just as important to watch the quantity of fats in your diet as it is to pay attention to the quality of fats in your diet. Keep your daily fat intake below 25 percent of your total energy intake for the day.

Below is a quick reference table that will help you learn about the different kinds of fats found in various oils. Generally, oils with fewer saturated fats and more unsaturated fats, especially the monounsaturated fats, are the best oils. For convenience, the different kinds of fats are expressed as P/S and P-M/S ratios.

	% Saturated	%Monounsaturated	%Polyunsaturated	P/S	P-M/S
Canola	7	56	33	4.9	12.7
Safflower	9	12	74	8.2	9.6
Corn	13	24	59	4.5	6.4
Olive	14	74	8	0.6	5.9
Soybean	14	23	58	4.1	5.8
Sesame	14	40	42	3.0	5.9
Cottonseed	26	18	52	2.0	2.7
Peanut	17	46	32	1.9	4.6
Palm	49	37	9	0.2	1.0
Palm Kernel	81	11	2	0.02	0.16
Coconut	87	6	2	0.02	0.09

For additional information on the nutrient content of selected foods, you may find it helpful to browse through the Food Composition Tables published by the USDA.

Are Nonfat Foods Fattening?

Let's learn about nonfat foods.

How many times have you seen the many magazine covers featuring amazing new diets or miracle remedies for weight loss?

I thought so.

These magazine articles invariably feature pictures of slim women or men next to low fat or nonfat foods. When viewed together, this combination of images sets off a powerful subliminal association.

The message is clear.

Eat nonfat foods and you will get slim.

What a powerful message to convey to someone who loves to eat and yet also would like to be thin.

Reality says something else: If you eat it and don't need it, you will wear it.

Don't misjudge this message—it's always a great idea to limit or restrict fat and calories to minimize the chance of gaining weight. But remember, generally speaking, a portion of the food you eat that you don't need will be changed by your liver into fat before being packaged, shipped, and displayed on your body.

Many people fall prey to the illusion that they are eating fewer total calories a day when they consume diet foods or lower fat foods. They think, incorrectly, that they are on a diet because the food wrapper has the word *diet* on it.

In many cases this proclamation of fewer calories on the label is sufficient to tempt the dieter's interest for another helping or serving. In essence, they mistakenly assume that they are protected from weight gain by eating diet or nonfat foods that have fewer calories spoonful for spoonful.

It's really not a mystery.

People will just eat more low fat or nonfat foods. And as they eat more, they gain more weight—it just takes more time and more spoonfuls to get the job done.

People in our society are heavier today than ever before. Approximately three out of four people in this country are overweight, despite the thousands of diets they go on and low fat foods they consume.

Incidentally, how many times have you seen a person eating a meat or cheese sandwich in one hand and holding a diet soda in the other hand, while they're watching a weekend of sports on television?

Remember, no one is dieting if they're eating a double bacon cheeseburger with a 64-ounce diet soda and some nonfat potato chips. You're dieting, however, when you make even the tiniest adjustments to your caloric intake. That's great news for not having to make huge lifestyle changes.

Next time you're thinking about eating the extra helping of nonfat dessert, you may want to remember that it's the *little* things that you eat or don't eat on a regular basis that will ultimately make the biggest difference in your weight.

Be Careful What You Take To Heart

Certain things should exist in your heart.
Love.
Compassion.
Kindness.
And forgiveness.
Other things should not be in your heart.
Stress.
Anger.
Resentment.
And certainly not the infamous cholesterol, which likes to hide amongst greasy artery clogging animal fats.

If you have been good to your heart and your heart has been good to you, then you probably don't think about it very often.

Days, weeks, and perhaps years may have passed without giving thought to what, "you've taken to heart." That's not unusual since the heart beats quietly about 100,000 times per day, usually without ever being heard.

There has never been a "pump" more amazing or forgiving than the heart. Despite stress, poor dietary habits, and sedentary living, it will beat about two and one-half billion times by the time a person turns 65 years old.

Now that's a miraculous performance by any standard.

Imagine, however, the results if we're a little extra careful about the things that we "take to heart."

Go ahead.

Do your heart good.

Treat yourself to a platter of fresh fruit wrapped with care and served with love.

You deserve it.

Lighten Up

A light heart lives long.

— Shakespeare, 1564-1616

The Ugliest Fat of All

The ugliest fat of all is the fat you can't see.

For many people, it's not only the extra fat they're wearing, but also the high levels of fat and cholesterol circulating throughout their blood system that is the most dreadful and threatening to their health.

So, let's get technical.

Blood fats are carried throughout your body with the help of a transporter or carrier system called lipoproteins. These various "transport vehicles" are specifically used to shuttle fats and cholesterol throughout your blood. The type and number of these transporters can be used to determine your risk of developing heart disease.

At times, blood lipids or fats act as "artery cloggers." All too often people significantly increase their risk of heart disease by eating too many rich, fatty foods. "Rich and creamy" blood is the result of devouring too much fat. All blood fats need assistance by lipoproteins to maneuver the fat and cholesterol through the blood.

Remember, not all lipoproteins are treated equal in terms of how they affect our chances of developing heart disease.

Lipoproteins have been given nicknames by biochemists and doctors. HDLs (high density lipoproteins) and LDLs (low density lipoproteins) are two lipoproteins frequently discussed in connection with the risk of developing heart disease. HDLs are referred to as "good" cholesterol and LDLs are referred to as "bad" cholesterol.

For years, doctors have known that a high LDL count indicates an increased risk of heart disease. In contrast, HDLs in greater quantities seem to significantly reduce that risk.

A screening can be performed to determine blood fat, total cholesterol levels, and the various types of lipoproteins carrying these lipids throughout your blood circulatory system.

Remember, you don't need to consume any cholesterol in your diet. When you need a little cholesterol to make some important biological compounds such as vitamin D, your body will manufacture sufficient amounts to meet your daily needs.

Give your heart a break, watch your diet and keep the ugliest fat of all out of your arteries.

It's Nowhere To Be Found

Have you ever looked for something in the wrong place, and sure enough, never found it there?

We all have.

Some things just belong in certain places, while other things belong somewhere else.

That's not unusual.

For example, if you go looking for cholesterol in plant products, you'll be searching for a very long time. That's because cholesterol, the infamous artery clogging compound, is only found in animals and animal products.

From the seemingly endless combinations of foods that we consume, there are only two original sources from which all foods are derived: plants and animals.

All plants have absolutely zero cholesterol.

Even nuts and avocados, which have a high fat content, have no cholesterol.

Zip.

Zero.

None.

All the cholesterol your body will ever need and use to make important bodily compounds, such as vitamin D, and male and female sex hormones, for example, is made from scratch in your liver.

Remember, the little difference is in knowing which foods contain cholesterol and which ones don't. The big difference is the healthy payoff your body gets when you actually eat foods with low or no cholesterol.

Where's the Cholesterol?

Food	Quantity	Cholesterol
Meat		
Beef, pork, lamb, etc.	1 oz.	25-28 mg
Poultry (w/o skin)		
Chicken, duck, turkey	1 oz.	22-25 mg
Fish		
Bass, cod, salmon, etc.	1 oz.	18 mg
Shellfish		
Crab, lobster	1 oz.	26 mg
Shrimp	1 oz.	42 mg
Organ tissue		
Liver (chicken)	1 oz.	208 mg
Milk products		
Whole (3.3% fat)	8 oz.	34 mg
Low fat (2% fat)	8 oz.	18 mg
Low fat (1% fat)	8 oz.	10 mg
Skim (nonfat)	8 oz.	4 mg
Cheese		
Cheddar	1 oz.	30 mg
Provolone	1 oz.	20 mg
Most average	1 oz.	25 mg
Egg(s)	1	220 mg
Fats and oils		
Butter	1 tbsp	31 mg
Margarine	1 tbsp	0 mg
Lard	1 tbsp	12 mg
Bacon fat	1 tbsp	84 mg
Vegetable oils	1 tbsp	0 mg
All plant products	any	zero

For additional information on the nutrient content of selected foods, you may find it helpful to browse through the Food Composition Tables published by the USDA.

Good Versus Bad Carbohydrates

In the simplest terms, there are two types of dietary carbohydrates.

Simple carbohydrates and complex carbohydrates.

Sweet or simple carbohydrates are called sugars.

Complex carbohydrates, such as starch and cellulose, which lack the sweet taste, often are called polysaccharides.

Virtually all carbohydrates, whether simple or complex, are obtained in your diet by eating plant products. People who love steak, ham, sausage, and eggs, and who don't care much for fruits, vegetables, and cereals, hardly get any carbohydrates in their diet at all.

Despite certain fad diets that lay claim to unsubstantiated benefits from eating low carbohydrate meals, carbohydrates should be one of the main nutrient groups that provides your body with approximately sixty percent of its daily energy needs.

But be careful.

You should be getting about five times more fuel energy from complex carbohydrates than from sugars. How can you estimate this ratio without pulling your hair out or using a calculator to do the mathematical calculations? Simply by not making meat and other animal products your main course, and eating more generous portions of a wide variety of vegetables, whole grain cereals, and fresh fruits.

Remember, both complex and simple carbohydrate foods are loaded with an abundance of healthy nutrients that are wholesome when they're found naturally in whole grain cereals, vegetables, and fresh fruits. Carbohydrates get their shoddy name and trashy reputation when they're found hiding in candy, doughnuts, chips, and other processed "junk" foods that are packed with sugar, salt, fat, preservatives, and empty calories.

So be smart.

Don't make the very common, but unfortunate, mistake of lumping all the carbohydrates together. Making no distinction between good and bad sources of carbohydrates not only is a big mistake, but also may be the rationale behind why many misinformed people support the infamous "low carbohydrate" diets.

Low carbohydrate diets mean one thing.

Poor choice.

Consuming a diet low in plants and high in animal products — which is the criteria of low carbohydrate diets — will increase your intake of cholesterol and saturated fats, decrease your fiber intake, decrease your intake of certain essential vitamins, and decrease your intake of potent phytochemicals or plant chemicals that are known to fight certain cancers.

This is not very good news if you're interested in reducing your odds of developing heart disease, certain cancers, and gastrointestinal disorders and ailments.

Shop wisely.

Choose foods that contain healthy carbohydrates, such as the ones found in fresh fruits and vegetables, and whole grain cereals.

Be thoughtful and outspoken.

Say goodbye to all the processed carbohydrates and sugary foods that have no place in your kitchen or in your body.

Always remember, the science and philosophy behind the concept of "Smart Weight Loss" has as much to do with encouraging a healthy lifestyle, as it does with helping you lose unwanted pounds. It's critical that you understand that the nutritional composition of your diet profoundly affects the quality of your health, just as your total caloric intake in relation to your caloric expenditures, ultimately determines the degree to which you will gain or lose weight.

Every Meal is Breakfast

Regardless of the time of day, whenever you eat a meal or nibble on a snack, something special happens.

You're having a *breakfast*.

The word breakfast is derived from BREAK FAST, which means ending or breaking a fast.

Each time you eat, a special hormone called insulin is normally released into your blood system. Once released, the hormone then "breaks the fast" by sending special biological instructions directly to your body cells notifying them that you have eaten.

It's interesting to note that insulin is responsible for both storing fat and forbidding fat cells from giving up their fat. In fact, each time you misbehave by eating too much food or munching on too many snacks, the extra insulin produced acts like *jail keepers* by temporarily locking up the fat in storage and tossing the keys away.

It comes down to basic math.

More food.

More insulin.

More fat.

When there's too much food, especially the wrong kinds of food in your diet, there are simply too many *jail keepers* bent on making, storing, and incarcerating fat inside your body. Incidentally, "sweets" are notoriously the worst villains for triggering the release of insulin and locking up fat inside fat cells.

So, if you're interested in booting some fat out of *jail*— then start paying closer attention to what and how much you're eating for *breakfast*. With a little effort the *jail keepers* will get the message and take some time off from work.

Here's to a healthier breakfast, lunch, and dinner.

Bon appetite!

But, don't forget to watch out for the "trigger treats."

Trigger Treats

We have just learned on the previous page that insulin plays a huge role in both storing fat and locking up fat inside adipose or fat tissue. On the next page we will discover insulin's essential role in carbohydrate metabolism.

For now, let's focus our attention on some of the worst "treats" known for triggering the release of too much insulin for your body's own good.

The most serious "trigger treat" offenders are actually the simplest and easiest to recognize.

Yes, sweets composed of sugar are the culprits. Whether the refined sugar is found in a can, bowl, bottle, or box, consuming sweets can do more than cause unwanted weight gain—they can cause you to lose teeth, and can cause unwanted swings in blood sugar and insulin levels that can lead to the "sugar blues."

Treat yourself, avoid "trigger treats."

Don't Sing the Sugar Blues

The prefix "hypo" implies a low level of something. The suffix "glycemia" refers to blood sugar levels. Therefore, hypoglycemia refers to a condition where a person's blood sugar level is low.

The most common form of hypoglycemia is a condition marked by low blood sugar as a result of producing too much insulin after eating certain foods.

It's normal to produce and release insulin into the blood after eating. In fact, eating food is the normal trigger to release insulin into the blood to do its job. The problem arises, however, when too much insulin is released into the blood after eating foods that are taboo.

Let's get a little technical.

Insulin is an important hormone with many diverse biological functions. Aside from its role in fat metabolism, it's responsible for moving just the right amount of blood sugar (after eating a meal) into the billions of hungry cells that make up your body.

In essence, insulin opens the cell *doors* so that sugar can pass into the body cells. The length of time the little cell *doors* remain open determines just how much sugar leaves the blood and enters the body cells.

Hypoglycemic individuals usually experience low blood sugar levels after eating sugary type foods that cause the release of too much insulin. Again, too much insulin release leads to less sugar in the blood.

The sugar in blood functions like gasoline in a fuel line that supplies energy to a car engine. A drop in the level of sugar can produce muscle weakness, HUNGER, sweating, dizziness, trembling, headache, and confusion, all of which make for an unpleasant and potentially dangerous experience.

It is important to always maintain appropriate levels of sugar in the blood. You may want to consult with your medical or health care professionals if you have any doubt about your ability to regulate blood sugar levels. Also understanding and knowing exactly which foods are problematic for the hypoglycemic is helpful in managing and avoiding unnecessary responses to these foods.

Furthermore, it's important to be careful not to confuse hypoglycemia with hyperglycemia, a major symptom of diabetes.

Diabetes is a disease or disorder in which insufficient amounts of insulin are produced after a meal or the insulin that is produced is ineffective. In other words, insulin is not doing the job it was instructed to do.

Clinically, there are two types of diabetes.

Type I diabetes, also known as insulin-dependent, growth-onset, or juvenile-onset, is much less common than Type II diabetes.

Type II diabetes, also called noninsulin-dependent, maturity-onset, or adult-onset, represents the most prevalent form of diabetes. About 80 percent of diabetics fall into this category. Type II diabetes is characterized by insulin resistance.

Some physiological symptoms of an untreated diabetic include hyperglycemia, glycosuria (glucose in the urine), polyuria (frequent urination), polydipsia (increased fluid intake), weight loss, and ketosis.

Depending on the type and severity of the diabetic's condition, proper diet, drug treatment and/or insulin may be needed to avoid high blood sugar or hyperglycemic states.

You Seem So Sweet—But You're Not

We have all been fooled by something at one time or another in our lives. It's not much fun being deceived—at any time. It's even more distasteful to learn that you've been duped by an impostor that seemed too sweet to be true, and wasn't.

In the world of nutrition, *pretenders* and *imitators* abound in many forms. Although they appear sweet on the surface, they are actually artificial sweeteners.

Don't be fooled.

Artificial sweeteners seem sweet, but they're not.

They're designed to deceive their true identity by fooling your tongue. Make no mistake, artificial sweeteners are very clever, but not smart enough to trick your brain.

Dieters beware!

At times, however, some people have become so gullible that they think they're on a special diet by simply holding a can of diet soda. Now that's a clever impostor by any standard.

Keep your senses.

Sure, the can of soda may have the word DIET on the label, but that does not mean you're on a diet. It means one thing. You're spending good money for a can or bottle of refreshment to either satisfy your thirst or quench your need for a little buzz or entertainment.

"Oh, how wonderful, all this hoopla in a can without any calories."

Ah!

Scientific research does not show a strong correlation or association between the consumption of artificially sweetened products and weight loss. With so many artificially sweetened products being consumed each day by millions of dieters, you might think these people would be thin, but they're not.

Sorry!

Fizzle.

Fizzle.

Question Myths

"Best is not always better."

Not So Good is Great

Let's blast a few common myths.

"More is better than less."

"Bigger is better than smaller."

Higher quality is always better than lower quality."

And, yes, "Chickens always come before the eggs," or, perhaps, "Eggs always come before the chickens."

Who really cares which came first, the chicken or the egg, if you're hungry and your attention is on preparing an egg salad sandwich for lunch?

Not me!

I would rather focus our attention on the nutritional value of chickens, eggs, and other animal sources of protein in your diet. For many people, the first foods that come to mind when they want to get the "best" proteins in their diet are meats, eggs, milk, and cheese.

This concept raises a question: Are proteins found in animals a better or higher quality source of proteins than proteins found in plants?

Yes and no.

Let's clarify the confusion so this age-old dilemma is put to rest, once and for all.

All proteins, both plant and animal, are made up of a mixture or combination of different building blocks, technically referred to as amino acids.

From a dietary perspective, there are basically two different kinds of amino acids.

Essential amino acids.

And *nonessential* amino acids.

Essential amino acids are very important to get in your diet, because your body cannot make them.

Nonessential amino acids are easily produced in a healthy body; therefore it's not essential to get them in your diet per say.

Remember, it is important to satisfy your requirement for essential amino acids. There is no need to consume any particular or specific kinds of protein. It is important, however, that most adults satisfy their daily need for amino acids by eating a variety of foods that contribute approximately 10 to 12 percent of their total calories from protein. Basically, this would represent about 50 to 60 grams of protein per day for an average adult consuming a 2,000 calorie diet.

Satisfying your need for the essential amino acids can be accomplished in a number of ways. One method is by simply eating high quality proteins from animal sources, called "complete" proteins. As you might expect, complete proteins have all of the essential amino acids in sufficient quantities to satisfy your amino acid needs.

Your need for essential amino acids also can be easily met by simply eating a variety of complementary lower quality plant proteins, often called "incomplete" proteins. Incomplete proteins earn their name because they are deficient or lacking in one or more of the essential amino acids.

So, who really cares how you satisfy your need for essential amino acids? You and your heart do.

Whenever you eat a variety of two or more lower quality plant proteins that complement or supplement each other so as to mimic the contents of a complete protein, then your body's need for essential amino acids is not only met, but you get a special nutritional bonus as well!

Some wonderful things happen when you start eating more plant based foods and less animal products—your intake of cholesterol and saturated fats decreases. Your intake of healthy fiber increases along with a healthful allowance of certain vitamins and minerals that are typically indigenous to plants. And, your intake of potent phytochemicals (plant chemicals) that help prevent and fight certain cancers, also increases.

Here's to you, to your heart, and to your health.

Where's the Protein?

Food	Quantity	Protein
Milk (whole, skim)	1 cup	8 grams
Cheese (most kinds)	1 oz.	6-7 grams
Yogurt (most kinds)	8 oz.	10-12 grams
Fish (most kinds)	1 oz.	5-7 grams
Meat (most kinds)	1 oz.	7-8 grams
Eggs	1 egg	6 grams
Bread (most brands)	1 slice	2-3 grams
Cereals (most brands)	1 cup	2-4 grams
Oatmeal (cooked)	1 cup	6 grams
Rice (cooked)	1 cup	4-6 grams
Egg noodles (cooked)	1 cup	7 grams
Nuts (most kinds)	1 oz.	6 grams
Cauliflower (chopped)	1 cup	2 grams
Carrots (raw, sliced)	1 cup	2 grams
Beans (lima, kidney)	1 cup	15 grams
Squash (cooked)	1 cup	2 grams
Fruits (most varieties)	1 cup	1 gram

For additional information on the nutrient content of selected foods, you may find it helpful to browse through the Food Composition Tables published by the USDA.

Relearn the Alphabet

The first letter of the alphabet is A.

The second is B.

Then comes C, of course.

D is next.

E follows nicely after D.

And so on.

We use these letters and some others not only to form words and add depth to our vocabulary, but also to name important vitamins.

Have you heard of vitamin A?

Sure you have.

What about vitamins B, C, or vitamin E?

There's no mystery to naming vitamins.

For ease and convenience, we customarily use letters of the alphabet to represent very impressive chemical names of vitamins.

It is just easier to say vitamin E than to say alpha-tocopherol. And it's just easier to say vitamin D than it is to pronounce 1,25-dihydroxycholecalciferol.

And so on.

Although a discussion of vitamins is well beyond the scope of this book, it's important to give credit and recognition to the vast number of vital and varied functions that vitamins play in our bodies. From releasing energy in foods, to building and maintaining the health of billions of body cells, vitamins, like minerals, are vital for life and good health.

Contrary to myth or wishful thinking, consuming extra vitamins or minerals, beyond your need or the established scientific recommendations, will not give you extra energy or help your body burn fat and lose weight.

Eat It—With a Grain of Salt

Beware.

Excessive salt consumption not only is a major culprit in exacerbating high blood pressure in millions of people, but salty foods also can arouse a person's appetite to new heights.

Natural fresh foods that are unprocessed are usually quite low in salt or sodium. In direct contrast, many processed foods are very high in sodium salts.

In general, the minimum recommended intake of sodium is 500 milligrams per day. The general recommendation for a healthy adult is between 1,000 and 3,300 milligrams per day. Interestingly, just one small teaspoon of table salt has two grams or 2,000 milligrams of sodium.

By not being diligent about your diet, your sodium intake can quickly become excessive.

So, be on your guard.

Eat only foods that have a tinge, smidgen, or trace of sodium here and there.

Salt of the Earth

Condiments	Portion size	Sodium (mg)
Salt (table)	1 tsp	2,000
Garlic salt	1 tsp	1,850
Fresh garlic	1 tsp	negligible
Soy sauce	1 tsp	1,030
Ketchup (regular)	1 tbsp	155
Mayonnaise (regular)	1 tbsp	80
Margarine (regular)	1 tbsp	140
Mustard	1 tbsp	65
Foods		
Most breads	1 slice	140
Cheese (Parmesan)	1 oz.	530
Cheese (Provolone)	1 oz.	250
Milk (whole/low-fat)	1 cup	120
Fresh fruit	any	negligible
Fresh vegetables	any	negligible
Most BK cereals	1 cup	200-500
Processed/canned	any	read labels
Meats (unprocessed)	3.5 oz.	65
Drinks		
Coffee	1 cup	negligible
Tea	1 cup	negligible
Sodas	12 oz.	read labels
Most beers	12 oz.	6-15
Most wines	3.5 oz.	5
Distilled spirits	any	0

For additional information on the nutrient content of selected foods, you may find it helpful to browse through the Food Composition Tables published by the USDA.

Cool Aids

Be cool.

Drink sufficient "cool aids."

Overheating and dehydration are actually more common than you might think, especially during the warmer climate seasons.

So, stay cool.

Simple pure water is certainly one of the best "cooling" aids known to satisfy your body's requirement for water and at the same time help rid your body of excess heat produced by the biological reactions occurring within your body cells.

Water is a precious nutrient.

It's found everywhere life flourishes.

It's interesting to note that virtually every biological process or reaction that's taking place inside us is occurring within cell fluids that total about two-thirds of our body weight. Certainly, we do not need to draw similarities between ourselves and mother earth, but it's worthy to mention that the earth's surface is covered with approximately two-thirds water. This vast environment of water not only is essential for sustaining the enormous population and variety of sea life, but also the diversity of life that dwells on land.

Okay.

Back to us.

The requirement for water intake varies significantly from person to person and from day to day. Factors that can influence your daily need for water include: degree of perspiration; high protein diets; starvation or low carbohydrate diets; untreated diabetic conditions; and vomiting and/or diarrhea.

In general, the "requirement" for water is related to the amount of water needed to offset the amount of water lost from the body. Because the actual requirement for water can greatly fluctuate, it's more convenient to suggest water recommendations.

Generally, for the average person, the recommendation for water intake is about one liter or quart of water per 1,000 calories of food energy consumed. Typically, about two-thirds of the water is actually derived from the beverages you drink and about one-third from the solid foods you eat.

Although an in-depth discussion of water and electrolyte (salts) replacement for athletes is well beyond the scope of this book, it's worth mentioning that very physically active people can easily lose up to several quarts of water per hour during very heavy exercise programs. Since water and electrolyte loss can impair heat tolerance, physical performance, and body function, it's very important for athletes to keep hydrated with fluids before, during, and after a physically strenuous event. Remember, it can be more of a science than an art to precisely determine the appropriate level of fluid and nutrient replacement for an individual during any stage of their activities.

Thirsty for more details?

Good.

Exercise physiology books are a great place to find detailed explanations and answers to any questions you may have about these important issues.

Remember, an adequately hydrated body is every bit as important for health and normal body function for the nonathlete as it is for a trained athlete.

More Waste—Less Waist

Interested in losing a few inches or more around your waist? Then you might want to think about getting more fiber in your diet. Research studies have shown that fiber-rich foods play an important role in weight management.

Why?

Because foods higher in fiber tend to be lower in calories, fats and sugars, take longer to eat, and promote a feeling of fullness.

If you search for fiber in meat and other animal products, you're going to come up empty-handed. That's because fiber only is found in plants.

Unprocessed fruits, vegetables, and cereals are great sources of healthy fiber. The more processed and refined the food, the less fiber will be found in the food.

Although there are many different kinds of fiber with funny sounding chemical names, let's keep this subject manageable by referring to the two main groups of soluble and insoluble fibers as simply dietary fibers. Also, for simplicity sake, let's refer to all undigested fiber that gets excreted from the body as waste.

You'll have to look elsewhere if you want to learn specific details about how various fibers earned their chemical names or how differently they work biologically in terms of exerting their specific effects on the body.

The overall health effects of fiber extend well beyond fiber's role in weight management. In general, dietary fiber plays extremely important roles in supporting the health of your heart and digestive tract, not to mention its role in the control of diabetes.

The next time you start noticing the inches coming off your waist, you'll appreciate the impact that fiber-rich foods have on other parts of your body.

Exchange Rates Made Simple

One ounce of alcohol contains 200 calories,
the caloric equivalent of six teaspoons of lard.

Fuel Award—Worst Runner-Up

When it comes to alcohol, size is not important.

Although alcohol is chemically only one-sixth the size of common table sugar, it is jammed with calories. Just one ounce of alcohol contains 200 calories, the equivalent of six teaspoons of lard. From a nutritionist's viewpoint, alcohol calories love to cling to our bodies.

Alcohol performs its dirty work by commanding the liver to make fat at a much faster rate than normal. When alcohol is broken down in the liver, powerful biochemical instructions are given to the liver to increase fat synthesis.

The liver listens very carefully.

Once fat is made in the liver, it is shipped out to be used or stored in adipose tissue.

Don't be fooled.

Even though alcohol may be clear like water, it looks very different on our bodies.

Aside from alcohol being incredibly fattening, it can become quite toxic to body cells and organs when consumed in sufficient quantities. Healthy bodies do not run well on poor quality fuels and alcohol is just that, a poor quality fuel. Although alcohol contains many calories, it has zero nutritional value. Moreover, alcohol is known to actually increase the need for certain nutrients. If things weren't bad enough, alcohol may also cause the unwanted excretion of some important nutrients.

In a society where the majority of folks are overweight and have no need for empty calories in their diet, alcohol continues to win the infamous *Worst Runner-Up Fuel Award.*

There is simply no glitz or glamour associated with receiving this runner-up award at a pageantry show where you're recognized for losing weight.

Don't Whine—Beer Isn't Any Better

Just how nutritious are alcoholic beverages? Well, an average adult would have to consume the following number of drinks every day to satisfy the need for the following nutrients for only one day!

Beer (12-ounce cans/day)	Wine (3.5-ounce glasses/day)
10 - 20 cans magnesium • riboflavin	20 - 40 glasses iron • magnesium
40 - 60 cans thiamine • calcium protein	180 - 350 glasses niacin • thiamine protein
80 - 120 cans iron • niacin	100 - 150 glasses zinc • calcium
130 - 170 cans zinc	40 - 60 glasses riboflavin

Distilled spirits provide virtually zero nutrition. Beer, wine, and distilled spirits are not a significant source of nutrients.

A Loss is Not a Defeat

*"Knowing what doesn't work is just
as important as knowing what works."*

Learn From Losers

Be open.
Be selective.
Be aware.

Although you can learn much about life and success from winners, you also can learn much from *losers* — losers of unwanted pounds that is!

Everyone has a story to tell about one thing or another. Which story and where you hear the story, however, is of utmost importance to you.

Sharing ideas and experiences with people who have successfully lost weight while still maintaining and promoting their overall level of health can be quite comforting, reassuring, and inspiring for anyone who wants a few extra personal tips from their friends, spouses, or like-minded associates.

One of the most important questions you can ask yourself before learning from a *loser* is whether he or she lost weight by subscribing to a diet and lifestyle change that was recognized, approved, or endorsed by a reputable national health or medical organization.

Since there are too many questionable and potentially dangerous diets to mention or list in this book, to further assist you, earlier in this book I mentioned some of the most highly regarded and reputable health and medical organizations in the country. Volumes of additional information on diets and health issues can easily be obtained by contacting these organizations.

Be curious.
Be diligent.
Be informed.

Flex Your Strength

I bend but do not break.

— Jean de La Fontaine, 1621-1695

Rigid Diets Usually Snap

"Only eat this."

"Never eat that."

"You must eat this before eating that."

"Don't ever eat this until you have finished eating that."

Have you ever felt a little exhausted or weary from trying to adhere to a strict manual of convoluted instructions that seem more like a maze than a sensible dietary and exercise program?

You're not alone.

A labyrinth of winding steps with twisting turns won't help you lose weight, it will only help you lose your sense of direction and balance, before you eventually lose your patience and mind.

Snap.

Snap.

It's no wonder that people become confused, lost, and abandon certain rigid or inflexible diets.

They're disoriented and bored stiff.

Remember, anything that won't bend will eventually buckle, break, and then bust into pieces. It just becomes a matter of time before rigid dietary regimens cause the dieter to crack as well.

There's absolutely no scientific foundation or merit to support special diets that lay claim to weight loss based on special food combinations with special timing requirements.

Paying attention to what you eat, how much you eat, combined with what and how much you move your body will give you the balance to manage your weight.

Snap yourself into shape.

Be flexible.

Don't Cycle

Cycling destroys muscle.

Routine cycling can make a person even fatter than before they started cycling.

Yet people continue to cycle.

Why?

Ignorance—maybe.

So what is *cycling*?

Cycling is a term used in the weight loss field whereby people first lose weight, then regain it, and then lose it again before regaining it all back again.

It's the up-and-down aspect of cycling that erodes a person's ability and desire to continue with their undulating and precarious cycle ride.

Cycling also is called "yo-yo" dieting.

Exhaustion and feelings of bewilderment usually reflect the sentiments of dieters who have won and then lost their battle with weight. The more times you lose weight, only to regain it, the more likely you will begin to associate feelings of failure with each weight loss cycle.

That's not unusual.

The key to avoiding the up-and-down cycles is to stay focused on strategies that bolster your metabolism, morale, determination, and ultimately your likelihood of success.

For starters, you may want to go bicycle riding instead of *cycling*. Physical activities that are fun, bring joy, and tone your muscles at the same time, will help battle the bulge and the ups and downs of cycling.

Life is full of exciting things to do.

Call a friend.

And ride your bicycle.

Happy trails.

Diets Designed and Destined To Destruct

Luck.

Chance.

And risk.

These three simple words may be all it takes to conjure up images of glitzy gambling casinos where the consequences of one's luck hinge on a toss of the dice.

Betting against house odds is typically unwise. Nor is it smart to wager a bet to lose weight when dealing with haphazard risky diets.

For the big and small rollers alike, the antes are too high and the stakes too important to play roulette with your body.

So, limit your losses and play smart.

Don't gamble.

Here are the rules and reasons why some diets are designed and destined to destruct:

Weight loss was too rapid.

The diet was imbalanced.

The diet caused too much muscle loss.

The diet caused the body metabolism to slow down.

The diet became boring and monotonous.

The diet was too rigid and emphasized deprivation.

The diet was high in fat and too low in carbohydrates.

The diet did not support or promote health.

An exercise plan wasn't considered.

No specific personal goals were established.

The diet lacked a reward system.

The dieter's emotions and beliefs were not considered.

And the diet was not specifically tailored to the dieter.

Hopefully, by appreciating and understanding some of the major reasons why diets are destined to fail, you will increase your odds of winning.

Here's to winning at losing—weight that is.

Crash Diets Cause Wrecks

Bang.

Clang.

Smash.

Crash.

These four words are probably the most unpleasant sounds anyone would ever care to hear or witness. Interestingly, even without ever being in an accident, some people wake up some mornings feeling mentally and physically like a *wreck*, or at least acting as though they've been through a *crash* or two.

Have you?

I hope not.

Well anyway, the aftermath of a *crash* diet will cause you to feel like a *wreck* virtually every time. Weariness, fatigue, weakness, and irritability are some of the early symptoms of food deprivation that can occur during a *crash* diet program.

Desperately trying to rapidly shed weight by starving your body on a very low calorie diet is tantamount to starvation.

Not fun.

And certainly unhealthy.

If you have ever tried a *crash* diet to quickly lose weight, then you probably know just what it feels like to be a physical and mental wreck.

Anyone can lose some weight on a *crash* diet, but who wants to compromise his or her strength, vitality, and health just to say, "I lost a few pounds"?

No one.

Be smart.

Don't cause a wreck.

The Truth Doesn't Change

*I only wish I could discover the truth
as easily as I can expose falsehood.*

— Cicero, 106-43 B.C.

The Yellow-Page Diet

Are you ready to try the New Exciting Miracle Diet that will not only change your entire life, but also will make you younger, stronger, happier, and even richer at the same time?

I'm sorry.

There is no such diet.

Wishful thinking about finding cure-all diets will only waste precious time.

I would, however, like to introduce you to a diet you haven't heard of until now—the Yellow-Page Diet.

It's a fictitious diet that I just contrived in my mind to demonstrate an important point about why certain fad diets should be vigilantly avoided.

So, even though the Yellow-Page Diet doesn't exist, here's how it would theoretically work if it were to exist.

Throughout the day you simply browse endlessly through the Yellow Pages.

Page after page.

Hour after hour.

Day after day.

Keep turning the Yellow Pages for a couple of days or until boredom numbs your mind. As you continue browsing through the Yellow Pages, drinking only water, the weight melts away.

What's so special about the Yellow-Page Diet?

Nothing!

It's an absurd and dangerous diet plan to follow!

Let's say it again.

It's an absurd and dangerous diet plan to follow!

I brought your attention to this ridiculous diet because there are some people who would actually think that the weight loss had something to do with reading the Yellow Pages. Obviously, the weight loss would have been due to food deprivation during the days you were browsing through the

Yellow Pages.

There are hundreds of diets just as silly and dangerous as this fictional Yellow-Page Diet, and they are all cleverly disguised by different names to entice you to try them.

So, be smart.

Be cautious.

The next time you hear about a NEW amazing diet, please check the Yellow Pages in your telephone book for information on where to locate the appropriate health or medical association that can steer you in the right direction.

The Big "M" Word

Let's debut one of the most important words in this book that affects every aspect of your body's function and chemistry, let alone your ability to manage and control your weight.

The big "M" word is *metabolism.*

Metabolism, in the broadest sense, means something will either be broken down to smaller pieces or little pieces will be hooked together to make something larger.

Let's summarize several hundred hours of college science courses in just a few sentences.

First, we eat food.

Then we break down the food into nutrients and energy.

After that, we use the energy and nutrients from the food we've eaten to build and maintain our bodies as we make our way throughout life.

All along the way, thousands of metabolic processes are occurring within every cell of your body to keep you alive. Interestingly, the rate or speed of your metabolism is one of several extremely important factors that determine how many calories your body burns each day.

The faster your metabolism, the faster you burn calories. The slower your metabolism, the slower you burn calories.

Your best line of defense against weight gain is to keep your body metabolism from becoming sluggish. A slothful metabolism is often caused by muscle loss, and muscle loss is the result of either rapid weight loss or physical inactivity.

Gradual weight loss minimizes the risk of destroying your body's natural defense against weight gain. Losing weight quickly sounds great, but it virtually guarantees disappointment and disillusionment with the battle against weight gain.

A common but huge mistake among dieters is to fixate on weight loss at any cost. Spurred on by any potential short-lived "success" they believe they are getting from a rapid weight loss program, these dieters unfortunately fail to ask the essential question: "What am I actually losing?" In reality, they're losing much more than what they bargained for on a rapid weight loss scheme, they're sacrificing:

Strength.

Stamina.

And potentially their health.

So, keep your senses.

Keep active.

Remember, before starting any exercise or physical fitness program it is very important to first consult with your physician.

The Roaring '20s

The 1920s were a special time in America, I'm told.

Yes, names that are as recognizable today as they were in the 1920s still surface in our memories from time to time.

Charlie Chaplin.

Duke Ellington.

Al Capone.

Rudolph Valentino.

Babe Ruth.

And, the fictional Mickey Mouse to name only a few.

How special the roaring twenties must have been.

For those of us past our twenties, our *Roaring '20s* are fading fast, too. I'm talking about your metabolism in your early to late twenties.

As the years pass, your metabolism is headed in a southerly direction.

That's life.

Is it possible to bring back your twenties when your metabolism hummed along at a nice clip?

No.

But there is one scientifically proven fact that explains why some people retain some of their own *Roaring '20s* well beyond their actual twenties.

Physical activity.

Muscle tissue stokes your metabolism.

In contrast, adipose tissue smothers your metabolism.

May I make a suggestion?

Move more.

Take a nice walk.

Regardless of the direction you choose to head, it's comforting to know that your metabolism will be headed north.

Lose While You Snooze

Is it possible to burn calories while you sleep?

Absolutely!

Whether it is day or night, we are all constantly burning calories. Some people, however, burn much more energy than others during the same period of time.

Here is how it works.

Regardless of whether you move your body, a huge portion of the food that you eat is burned up each day just to keep you alive. Depending on your physical size and your level of fitness, you may be burning roughly 60 calories per hour lying around doing absolutely no physical activities.

Actually, when you think you're doing nothing while you're resting or snoozing, in reality, your body is very busy pumping blood, breathing, maintaining body temperature, and much more.

Interestingly, the energy required to just keep you alive during physical, emotional, and digestive rest is referred to as your *basal energy needs* or *basal metabolism*. Without regard to age, sex, size, or level of fitness, most adults expend approximately one calorie per minute for basal energy expenditures. Although this number is influenced by many factors, your total body muscle mass is one of the most important factors determining the amount of calories you can burn day in and day out while at rest.

With a little math, you can see that an average adult expends about 500 calories during an eight-hour night's rest.

The less muscle you have, the less calories you will burn while you rest. In contrast, the more muscle you have, the more calories you will burn while you rest.

It's comforting to know that the more muscle you maintain by being physically active during daylight hours, the more calories you'll be burning while you snooze.

Not a bad deal for a honest day's work.

Slow Down and Burn Some Fat

Let's talk about burning fat.

You may be surprised to learn that your body burns proportionately less fat as you increase the intensity of your physical workouts. And we all know what happens when we exert ourselves too much and too quickly.

Yes, our breathing rate increases dramatically.

Biologically, it's impossible for muscles to burn fat unless they receive enough oxygen. Consequently, if your heart is racing and your lungs are rapidly expanding and contracting from fast breathing, your muscles start burning proportionately less fat.

The basic law that determines whether fat is being burned is quite simple. Fat, like fireplace logs, cannot be burned without oxygen present. If you have ever fanned a fire to get it started, you'll recognize that it's the same concept.

The next time you exercise with the intent to burn fat, keep the intensity down and the duration up. This minor adjustment will allow your heart and lungs to deliver the necessary oxygen to your muscles.

There are two basic types of exercise: *aerobic* and *anaerobic* exercise. Aerobic literally means "in the presence of oxygen." Muscles are at their best when they have plenty of oxygen. Anaerobic, on the other hand, refers to an activity where there is a shortage of oxygen.

We must continually breathe oxygen to live, regardless of the activities we do. That's not big news.

In a sense, however, we're always doing aerobic activities—washing the car, taking a walk, working at the office, or reading this book. Right?

Occasionally, however, we'll do something that gets our heart and breathing rate up. Perhaps a jog, a mountain climb, or a game of tennis is all it takes to elevate our heart and breathing rate. The activity remains aerobic if you're not straining for a breath of air. It's under these conditions that your body is *tuned* to burn fat for a longer period of time.

Activities become anaerobic when your body muscles are exercised so hard that the demand for oxygen makes it difficult to sustain the activity without gasping for air. The burning sensation you feel in your muscles during anaerobic exercise, such as lifting a weight many times, is caused by the accumulation of lactic acid. Lactic acid is the metabolite or end product formed from incompletely burning the sugar "glucose" within muscle tissue when there's an oxygen deficit caused by sustained muscular activity.

The increase in heart rate, breathing rate, and lactic acid production is a gauge of how hard your muscles are working and how proportionately less fat you're burning.

So, slow down a little bit. Have some fun.

The next time you start to get out of breath, you'll know the real reason why you should slow your pace a little bit.

Let's make one more point absolutely clear.

For the individual who prefers higher intensity physical workouts, you'll be interested to learn that ultimately more total energy (including calories derived from fat) can potentially be burned with more intense exercise; assuming, however, you are able to sustain the more strenuous activities for at least as long as you would be performing the same activity at a lower intensity level. In other words, you will always burn more total calories during more intense workouts than with less intense workouts; provided, however, you are able and willing to "go the distance" for the same length of time.

Ultimately, for a more accurate reflection of total energy expenditure of an individual—including the actual percentage of all fuels burned—one must understand that total caloric utilization from individual fuels is not only a function of frequency, duration, type of activity, and level of physical exertion or intensity, but also a function of an individual's age, body weight, health, and physical condition.

Don't Let Your Genes Determine Your Pant Size

It's common knowledge that obesity runs in certain families. Special molecules in the nucleus of cells, called deoxyribonucleic acid, or simply DNA, house huge volumes of genetic information that allows physical traits to be passed on from one generation to another. All of us inherit certain "genes" or genetic endowments that determine which biological instructions will be used to guide our physical development from the color of our eyes to the size of our nose.

Inheriting a "bundle of traits" that instructs certain people to gain "fat" weight more easily than another person is certainly another way genetic information makes its presence noticed.

The real question is not whether genetics plays a role in obesity, but rather, to what extent?

Genetic instructions that alter a person's ability to burn calories by only 1 PERCENT can spell weight gain across the hips, butts, thighs, and stomachs of many dieters. Biological factors coupled with environmental factors such as nutrition, exercise, and lifestyle choices work together to determine exactly how much weight will be gained over time.

You can buy your pants anywhere, but you only can get your "genes" from one source.

Your parents.

So, if for any reason you're unhappy with your "genes," you can still drop your pant size by exercising your body more frequently and exercising good nutritional judgment more regularly.

Scales Don't Tell the Whole Truth

Scales are great for measuring one thing—your weight.

Although scales are useful to determine how heavy you are, they tell us nothing about other important things you need to know, such as:

Stamina.

Body shape.

Bone strength.

Blood pressure.

Body composition.

And other vital things that determine your overall level of physical health and fitness.

Monitoring and maintaining good health as you manage your weight loss is every bit as important to your well-being as the benefits gained by losing unnecessary pounds.

Tip the scale in your favor—learn everything you can about healthy lifestyle changes that can't be weighed or measured by scales.

Gaining Fat Without Gaining Weight

Could you imagine having a great physique or figure with an ideal body weight and still be too fat? Millions of people are maintaining their weight, yet are becoming fatter and fatter each year.

Is it possible?

Absolutely!

Typically as people become more sedentary with time they lose muscle tissue and gain fat tissue.

The math is simple.

If you gain 10 pounds of fat and lose 10 pounds of muscle, you have essentially maintained your weight. This is why weighing yourself on a scale provides you with limited information about your body composition. A full-length mirror, although somewhat useful as a visual cue, also is limited in offering information or assessment of your body composition.

The terms "overweight" and "underweight" not only are overused, but are a bit outdated and misunderstood. To better appreciate this idea, imagine for a moment a person who is not overweight or underweight for their height, but who unfortunately has a huge excess of body fat disproportionately found in his or her rear end and belly. Essentially, for this person to have the correct weight for their height, they would have to have very skinny arms, shoulders, and legs.

Again, the two issues are: What are you composed of in terms of the percentage of fat and muscle? And where is the fat and muscle located in your body?

Maybe what you really want is a change in where you carry your weight. Perhaps less on the hips and waist and more in the shoulders and back muscles. Making a change in your shape, rather than necessarily changing your weight, may be more of an exercise issue than a diet matter. Diet without exercise will not encourage muscle growth.

The problem arises when we become physically inactive

as we get older. With inactivity, we not only compromise our ability to maintain our weight, but we also lose physical strength and endurance. Gaining weight in the form of fat becomes easier and easier because with each passing year most of us lose muscle tissue from the "good life" inactivity syndrome. Maintaining or building muscle by staying active is one of the single most important things you can do to stay healthy, trim, and feeling great.

The process of losing muscle and gaining fat is usually very subtle and not noticed until one day you are physically tested to do something that requires endurance and strength. It's this slow gradual change in body composition that is predominantly responsible for the slow but progressive gain in body fat, meal after meal, year after year.

To emphasize this point, let's talk about two people both weighing 200 pounds and both on a sedentary vacation doing little more than reading and watching television. Let's assume that one person is in great physical shape from regular exercise and the other person out of shape from inactivity. The person who is in good physical shape will be able to eat much more food each day than the other person if they are to both maintain their weight. It's the large body muscles, not fat tissue, that burn so much more of the food calories that we eat each day.

So if you are not overeating, and you find it difficult to lose fat weight, your body may be trying to tell you that you're getting out of shape as you age.

Ouch.

As we age, our bodies change in many ways. It almost goes without saying that gaining fat without gaining muscle is just too easy. In contrast, gaining muscle without gaining fat requires balanced nutrition along with regular physical exercise.

Be smart as you age, lose the fat pounds and add the muscle pounds. The key ingredient is simple.

More movement!

Sizing You Up

Aside from glancing in the mirror, one of the easiest methods used to determine how much extra weight you're carrying is to determine your BMI or body mass index.

Two things are required to calculate your BMI.

Know your weight in pounds.

Know your height in inches.

Now, do a little math using the formula below:

BMI = Weight (pounds) divided by height (inches)^2 times 705.

For instance, if you wanted to determine a person's BMI who weighs 150 pounds and who happens to be five feet, seven inches tall, you would simply square 67 inches (67 x 67 = 4,489) and then divide this number by 150 to arrive at 0.033. Next, multiply 0.033 by 705 to arrive at a BMI of 23.5 for this person.

The National Institutes of Health's guidelines define adult obesity with a score above 30; overweight between 25 to 29.9; normal weight between 19 to 24.9; and underweight scoring lower than 19.

Although determining your BMI is a useful tool to gain additional insight about your weight, it's worthy to note that the BMI index does not clearly distinguish between muscle weight and excess fat weight. Consequently, a well conditioned weight lifter may find that his or her BMI scores may be skewed too high and therefore not adequately represent a true weight assessment.

For the rest of us, short of glancing in the mirror, the body mass index scores can size us up quite quickly.

Hang On to Your Best Friends

Hello and welcome.

Please meet one of the best friends you'll ever have to help you burn fat 24 hours a day.

Your muscles!

Lean, strong muscle tissue will always assist you in losing unwanted pounds. If you aren't carrying extra pounds, then you have your muscles to thank.

Here's how it works.

Muscle tissue thrives on burning energy—especially when you put your muscles to work. Unlike fat tissue, muscle burns lots of energy, even when your muscles are resting. Fat tissue, on the other hand, thrives on storing energy.

Keep it simple.

Keep the muscle.

Lose the fat.

The more fat you wear, the more fat cells love to be fed because they have a ravenous appetite for maintaining their physique. As you can see, a vicious cycle of weight gain may ensue if fat cells are allowed to call the shots. If you become inactive, your fat cells will work overtime to turn you into chubby balls.

In addition to exercising, the best way to keep your muscles from shrinking is to lose any unwanted weight very slowly.

Don't lose weight too quickly.

Losing weight too rapidly destroys valuable muscle tissue that acts as powerful fat burners. Focus on losing body fat, not on losing muscle and body tone. At this rate, you and your muscles will both be happy.

Hang on to your best friends.

Give them what they need most—a regular workout.

Get Even First

Let's be honest.

At certain times in life it just seems like we have to "get even" or do whatever it takes to "clear the air" before we can start feeling better about the little things that irritate or agitate us.

This principle applies to many aspects of our lives.

When it comes to losing weight you're also going to have to GET EVEN before you can GET AHEAD.

GETTING EVEN first means getting your weight under control or stabilized so that at the very least your weight is not heading in an upward spiral.

The concept is much like throwing a ball above your head. After the ball is thrown straight up into the air, it must make a brief pause before it changes direction and falls back to you.

It's not rocket science.

It's just common sense.

If you're a little eager about losing rather than just maintaining your weight, then this wonderful feeling of "getting even" won't last very long.

The GETTING EVEN phase of weight loss, at the very least, means that during this time period, your brain is developing an understanding of how much food and activities it takes for you to maintain your weight without gaining any more pounds.

It may sound simple, but just learning how much food is required to maintain your weight without gaining weight is an important first step in weight management.

To help this process you'll need to pay very close attention to how much you are eating and how much you're moving. Keeping an accurate food and activity log is quite helpful.

Be diligent.

Be focused.

And be patient with yourself.

It took some time to gain weight, now it's going to take some time to lose that weight.

Okay, it's time to get even.

Grab a note pad and start writing down detailed notes about your diet and your level of physical activity for at least several days. The idea is to get acquainted with the types of food you're eating and the level of activity in which you're engaged. You will find that it doesn't take much time to spot the troublesome foods. Nor will it take much effort to identify how active or inactive you are throughout the week.

The entries into your log book or note pad are helpful tools to remind yourself of just what you're eating and doing. The data can be painful, but it keeps you honest.

With a little patience and study you not only will relearn how much food and activity you require to maintain your present weight, but more importantly you will discover just how much food and activities you require to lose the weight you desire.

Keeping food and activity logs may initially seem like a small step along the road to weight loss, but they're actually a huge leap in the right direction of weight management.

Good luck.

And remember, GETTING EVEN means more than just getting your weight in check, it means you have learned an important physics lesson.

The lesson is simple.

The quickest way to make a complete change in any direction, is to first come to a stop, get even at least temporarily, and then turn around and head in the new direction.

Here's to getting even.

Is Exercise for Everybody?

For most people, yes.

For some folks, no.

The fundamental goal of exercise is to promote physical fitness and health. Surely, no one should ever intentionally or unintentionally put themselves at risk for injury or jeopardize their well-being by engaging in an exercise or diet program that would not be tolerated because of some existing illness or medical condition.

Typically, should there be any doubt about one's physical condition it is wise to first consult a physician before starting any exercise program or engaging in any demanding physical activities.

The general purpose of health "screening" is to identify individuals who may have a medical condition that would make it unsafe to exercise, need special assistance in order to exercise, require a medically supervised exercise program, or need additional medical evaluation, treatment, or recovery time before starting an exercise program.

Be smart.

Be safe.

Be knowledgeable.

Know and respect your physical abilities and limitations.

Who Needs To Climb Mount Everest?

For some people physical activity conjures up images of work, sweat, and sore muscles.

For others, physical activity evokes other images:

Vibrance.

Vitality.

Vigor.

Zeal.

Zing.

Zest.

And zip.

Physical fitness is the condition of the body that determines its ability to perform various physical activities. For many years, physical fitness referred to a person's capacity for movement. In the narrowest sense, physical fitness relates to your ability to not only maneuver, but to also compete in a variety of athletic events.

The great news is you don't have to compete in competition or climb Mount Everest to be physically fit.

The term health-related physical fitness is used more often to stress the importance of physical activity to enhance health, endurance, strength, flexibility, longevity, and to decrease the risk of disease, disability, and premature death.

For most of us, the goal of physical fitness does not include running the fastest race or hitting the most baseballs in a season. It does, however, mean developing and maintaining a lifestyle with activities that promote health, happiness, and a positive attitude.

The old saying, "Go take a hike," may have more relevance to losing weight than what we once originally thought.

In any event, give it a try, it's fun.

Where Can I Find a Minute to Exercise?

Congratulations.

You have found some time in your busy schedule to start reading this page. But, more importantly, will you be able to find a few extra moments today to exercise?

I know with your busy schedule that your allotment of free time is quite sparse. Welcome to the group of busy bees, you're not alone.

So, where can you start looking for any extra free time? Well, virtually anywhere and at any time you want!

You have many choices each day to find a minute to move, stretch, or exercise your body. To be exact, you have 1,400 minutes or chances to start moving your body a little bit more each day.

Go ahead.

Try stretching or exercising a few small muscle groups for an entire 60 seconds.

Stretch your legs, arms, or back for just a minute. You'll still have 1,439 minutes left over to do other things today.

Benjamin Franklin once said, "If we take care of the minutes, the years will take care of themselves."

That's powerful!

So, whether you choose to spend a minute or two stretching, practicing relaxation techniques, or taking a few extra minutes to walk around the block, you'll begin to understand the power each moment holds in your life.

Get started.

Take a few minutes in your day and use them to make a big change in your life. Remember, before starting any exercise or physical fitness program it is a good idea to first consult with your physician.

The 2-Percent Factor

Is it possible to be sedentary most of the time and still greatly improve your health and physical shape by exercising less that 2-percent of the time?

Certainly!

There are 168 hours in a week.

And yes, it is true that several hours only represents a tiny fraction your week.

What can we accomplish in so little time?

Plenty.

Doctors have known for years that the general health of the heart, and the accompanying arteries that feed the heart, can be greatly improved by doing 30-minute aerobic workouts on all or most days of the week.

We don't have to swim the English Channel or climb to the top of Mount Everest to enjoy the benefits of a healthy heart and a firmer body.

If you're like most people, you don't like to exercise or can't find the time to exercise. If so, it then may be comforting to remember that you will still have about 165 hours each week to recover from any of your weekly exercise sessions.

Before beginning any exercise or physical fitness program it is very important to first consult with your physician.

So, do your body good.

Stretch it.

Bend it.

Move it.

Be good to it.

Please refer to the Appendix at the end of this book for a more precise and detailed explanation of the current suggested Guidelines for Physical Activity.

Soft On the Inside—Hard On the Outside

Kindness.
Tenderness.
And gentleness.
Yes, these words all evoke elements of a caring, giving, and loving soul.
On the other hand.
Big biceps.
Colossal calves.
And rippling stomach muscles conjure up images of what we like to call a "hard body" or physically fit body.
Incidentally, the blood vessels that feed and nourish strong body muscles can be analogized to feelings, in that blood vessels need to be soft, flexible, and giving, so that your heart won't have to be weakened by overworking under any undue harmful pressure.
So, keep it simple.
Be like an egg—be soft on the inside and hard on the outside. With a little effort each day, you can be soft, nice, and firm—just in the right places.

Pillars of Fitness

*"Strength, flexibility, and endurance
are the three pillars of physical fitness."*

Be Flexible With Your Strength

You are as strong as your weakest link.

Strength without flexibility is restrictive.

Flexibility without strength is limiting.

Strength and flexibility without endurance is confining.

Strength, flexibility, and endurance are the three pillars of physical fitness.

Your muscular strength refers to the maximum force that you can produce by an individual muscle or group of your muscles working together.

There are three general types of muscles: cardiac muscles (which pump blood); smooth muscles (which change, for instance, the volume of the stomach, intestines, and uterus); and skeletal muscles (which change the angle of bones).

Here are a few tips to increase your strength to move, lift, hold, push, or pull things.

Always slowly warm up before any workout.

Stretch before all workouts.

Never train to the point of causing pain.

Always use proper technique and equipment.

Exercise all muscle groups.

Use a full range of motion.

Breathe continuously—never hold your breath.

Get adequate rest—it is just as important as activity.

Curtail activities when you are ill.

Stay informed by learning.

Know and respect your physical limits, abilities, and current physical and medical condition.

Now, a few things about your joints. Joint flexibility is one aspect of physical fitness that is too often ignored or neglected. In simple terms, flexibility is the ability to move a joint through a full nonrestricted range of motion without incurring discomfort, pain or injury.

Stretching exercises are specifically designed to improve

flexibility, increase the range of motion and reduce the risk of injury. Here are a few simple tips to increase your level of flexibility.

Slowly stretch to the point of tightness, never to the point of pain. Never bounce back and forth to get a stretch.

Use caution when stretching neck and lower back muscles, as well as muscles near painful joints.

Stretch a minimum of several times a week.

Learn proper techniques from illustrated books from reputable sources. Whenever you have any doubts or concerns about stretching your body, immediately seek professional advice.

The third pillar of physical fitness is muscular endurance. Muscular endurance is the ability of your muscle, or group of muscles, to contract over and over again for an extended period of time or until the muscle fatigues. Many people are generally interested or concerned with their cardiorespiratory (heart and lungs) endurance.

Cardiorespiratory, or simply cardiovascular endurance, is your ability to persist in a physical activity for an extended length of time. Running, swimming, climbing or rowing for extended periods could certainly impose a demand on your cardiovascular, respiratory, and skeletal muscle systems. Compared to all the elements of fitness, nothing is more important than your cardiorespiratory endurance.

Your heart and lungs are two very important organs that are responsible for continuously delivering the oxygen and nourishment to the hundreds of muscles and vital organs throughout your body.

The benefits of a healthy and strong cardiovascular system are phenomenal and the major benefits from improving your level of cardiovascular endurance will be enjoyed by your whole body.

Please Don't Eat and Run

Some people are always in a big rush!

For whatever reason, it's hard for them to sit still for very long.

How many times have you heard someone say, "Sorry, I have to run"?

Although I sometimes feel the need to "eat and run," I don't run or exercise until my meal has been digested. Eating and then immediately running or exercising just doesn't make good sense.

So, the next time you feel the need to suddenly "dine and dash," relax and give your body the time it needs to work on the food you've just eaten before you scoot.

Don't be in a hurry.

Eat.

Digest.

And then *run*.

This simple practice will give your body a chance to absorb and deliver the important nutrients and fuels to your muscles so they have a little extra energy to run on.

Pain—No Gain

Let's get smart.

Dump that old workout slogan "No Pain—No Gain."

It's outdated.

Subscribing to the philosophy "No Pain—No Gain" can potentially cause additional injuries and pain to your body.

Usually, the stronger the pain the louder the message.

If you feel any pain from exercising too rigorously—listen carefully, the pain is speaking to you in the most basic language.

Ouch.

Ouch.

Ouch.

You're hurting me!

Usually, any initial pain will get a person to stop the activity, action, or motion causing the pain.

Pain is an important physiological message that is sent racing from the point of injury in your body directly to your brain.

The message is simple.

Stop.

Get some rest.

Get some medical advice or attention if warranted.

And yes, give your body the time necessary to recover from the injury and yourself the time to think about whether the injury could have been avoided in the first place.

Remember.

Exercising improperly or training to the point of pain increases the risk of serious injury.

The next time you start to hear a squeak, creak, or screech in your knee, elbow, or limb, you'll know that the person who coined the slogan "No Pain—No Gain" probably meant to say "No Pain—No Gain—No Brain."

Ouch.

Take Your Eye Off the Ball

Billions of hours are spent each year watching balls hit, kicked, shot, and caught.

Whether it's preseason or playoff season there's certainly no shortage of sports enthusiasts who habitually follow the unfolding drama of sports as their favorite athletes and teams fight their way to the finish line.

Following and supporting players in various games and leagues throughout the different seasons can be quite time-consuming and at times quite exhausting, especially when the viewer has developed an emotional investment in the outcome of a particular game or series.

So, why do so many people devote astronomical amounts of their time watching balls moved from one place to another? Maybe because it's entertaining or because it's just human nature to want to watch opposing players or teams compete. Or perhaps the answer is as simple as trying to satisfy our desire to identify with the concept of success or winning. Surely, most of us are taught at an early age that in order to win or be successful we have to look straight ahead and attentively "keep our eye on the ball."

Great advice, but unfortunately some people have taken the suggestion too far. Spending enormous amounts of spare time watching balls hit, kicked, and caught won't even help you get to first base.

May I make a small suggestion?

To get a chance to compete at winning or occasionally hitting that "home run," you're going to have to make a few tiny changes.

First, turn off your TV set!

Challenge yourself to bend, stretch, or move your body long enough to equal ONE percent of the time you usually spend gazing at the flying balls on your TV.

Find your own ball.

Call a friend.

It's your turn to toss, roll, or catch a ball or two.

Go ahead, challenge yourself to burn up some of those *couch* calories. You can't miss if you take your eye off the ball for awhile.

Take It Off in Public

Don't be embarrassed.

It's perfectly natural—and legal.

And it can be done anywhere in public without offending anyone.

You decide on the details.

When.

Where.

And yes, you decide how much you're going to shed.

Are you ready to go outside?

Good.

Public grounds are a perfect place to shed or take off some extra body fat.

Playgrounds are awesome.

Walking and bicycle trails are a lot of fun, too.

And don't forget city parks.

Using indoor treadmills, stationary bicycles, and other mechanical devices are great ways to burn fat indoors, but their continued use can lead to a little claustrophobia.

The next time you're thinking about "taking it off"—get some fresh air at the same time.

With a little experience taking some pounds off outside, you'll not only be getting fresh air, but quite possibly a fresh new look.

So, take off some extra fat in public!

Go Fly a Kite

Quite frankly, I have come to believe that most people do in fact have good intentions in their hearts, despite differences or disagreements they have with each other.

So, the next time you share a brilliant idea with someone and they tell you to "go fly a kite," do it.

It's fun.

And it makes for a perfect excuse to get yourself outdoors so you can move your body and in the process burn a few extra calories.

Had I only taken the advice of my adversaries when they all told me to "take a hike," I would have been in phenomenal physical shape.

Hiking is great exercise for people who love adventure and are equipped to handle the trails.

Seriously.

Whatever your likings and abilities may be, remember to heed the good intentions of people who occasionally tell us to "fly a kite." They're not insulting us, they're simply reminding us, if even unknowingly, that we need to be more active.

So, go fly a kite.

Here's to the power of positive thinking.

And to getting your heart rate up a little bit!

Calculate Your Training Heart Rate

Are you interested in determining your Estimated Training Heart Rate?

Good.

Start by simply subtracting your age from 220 to arrive at your Estimated Maximum Heart Rate (EMHR). Then, multiply your EMHR by the percentage intensity factor (from the chart below). The resulting number is your Estimated Training Heart Rate.

Step One:

220 - Age = Estimated Maximum Heart Rate (EMHR)

Step Two:

EMHR) x (% Intensity Factor) = Estimated Training Heart Rate

Level	Beginner	Intermediate	Advanced
Duration	20 min.	30-45 min.	45-60+ min.
Frequency	3x / week	4-5x / week	5-6x / week
Intensity	60 %	70 %	75-80 %

Note: Generally the % Intensity Factor ranges from 0.6 (Beginners) to 0.8 (Advanced). Also note that the intensity factor may be set WELL BELOW 60% for some individuals with any health, fitness, and medical issues and concerns. Before starting any exercise or physical fitness program it is a very good idea to first consult with your physician.

Nonprescription Medicine

Walking is man's best medicine.

— Hippocrates, 460-377 B.C.

Super Bowl XL

Many of us are fascinated with "super bowls."
That's not unusual.

But let's be clear about "super bowls." Not all of them involve two world class football teams battling each other on a grassy field for the thrill and glory of being crowned champions.

Some "super bowls," especially the extra large or XL bowls, have more to do with cookware and serving dishes than sports. Yes, the "super bowls" that I'm referring to are those enormous oversized dishes that are so large that they can hold enough food to feed a small army. And yes, sometimes these dishes are unfortunately used in place of good old-fashioned dinner plates.

I can understand the dilemma associated with using big bowls. On the one hand, you're interested in losing weight. On the other hand, it's just too wonderful to have full access to an entire meal in a single dish, especially if your meal is going to be eaten sitting comfortably in front of your television. Just think about the amount of energy conserved by not having to get up and down several times for second helpings.

Seriously.

Here's a little helpful point.

If you're thinking about losing weight, try first thinking about smaller food portions. Remember, a huge plate or bowl can make even a large serving look small.

It may seem like a small difference, but just using smaller bowls and plates at meal times may give you the winning edge to lose weight.

Downsize

One of the most important elements of a successful weight loss program is understanding portion size.

With so many restaurants, food chains, and fastfood drive-thru establishments vying for your business, it's no wonder that special offers are aimed directly at your appetite.

Bargains come in many shapes and sizes.

Jumbo this—jumbo that.

Tall this—tall that.

Extra this—extra that.

And we've all heard the saying, "Supersize me."

These teasers may seem appealing at first glance, but most of us don't need the extra calories that accompany the "supersized" meal deals.

Portion size is key to your body's size.

Here are the rules:

Supersize if you want to gain a size.

Downsize if you want to drop a size.

Remember, portion control is just another way of saying self-control.

Exercise Poor-shun Control

Learning about the importance of portion control is half the battle when it comes to curbing your intake of extra calories. Restricting the consumption of poor quality foods also is every bit as important to your weight and health as limiting too much food in your diet.

The next time you exercise portion control, go the extra mile and practice "poor-shun" control.

It's easy to do.

If the food is poor quality, simply shy away from it. Generally, foods loaded with sugar, salt, and fat, that are lacking in nutrient content are poor quality foods. In very little time you'll be practicing "poor-shun" control without giving it much thought.

Here's to improving your diet before you serve yourself a helping or portion of food.

Banana Split

Some truths are self-evident.

Most desserts are crammed, packed, and stuffed with pudgy, portly, paunchy fats.

Banana splits are no exception.

They're swollen with rich, creamy calories.

Yum

Yum.

So how can a banana split help you lose weight? Listen carefully to the message hidden in its name.

It's crying out a warning to you.

"Split me."

"Share me."

And if you're mindful and heed this advice, the probability of eating one-half the calories in a banana split or some other dessert will approach 100 percent.

Ah, the bliss of the old adage, "Share and share alike."

For special effects, start sharing entrees.

Lunch Hour Shouldn't Be Munch Hour

During a regular five-day workweek, most people get an hour a day for lunch. This ritualistic practice of taking a "lunch hour" each day usually begins on Monday and ends on Friday.

That's not unusual.

People who use the whole lunch hour to eat may as well rename their lunch hour, the "munch hour."

Personally, I like to refer to "lunch hour" as the lunch BREAK. Using the word BREAK is just a gentle reminder for me to stop, pause, and reconsider if I really want to devote the entire 60 minutes to eating.

Try something different.

Take only 30 minutes of time to eat.

This will leave you with 30 whole minutes each day to burn and walk off part of your lunch.

In very little time you'll notice a big difference in how you look, feel, and ultimately how much you weigh when your lunch hour becomes a lunch break.

If you're feeling enthusiastic and are looking for another way to squeeze some time out of each day to move or exercise a little, you might also consider giving your "dinner hour" a new name.

Give yourself a break.

Break your lunch and dinner hours in half.

Candy Bar

The word "bar" has more than 20 different meanings in the English language. In the context of our discussion of weight loss and diet, it has only one meaning: to exclude or keep out.

Yes.

The word "bar" when used in conjunction with the word candy, as in "candy bar," means or translates to a subliminal message that urges you to keep candy and other sweets out of your diet.

Open your eyes.

Open your ears.

Candy bars are speaking to you.

Listen carefully to their message.

They're offering sage advice.

Stay away.

Since there is absolutely no room for empty sugar and fat calories in a healthy diet, it may be best for you to leave the candy bars on the grocery store shelf.

The benefits are twofold.

Over time you'll be pounds lighter by not eating the candy, and secondly, any spared candy bars that remain on the grocery store shelves can continue to proudly display their message "ban me" to other shoppers tempted to buy and eat them.

Drive -Thru Restaurants

Have you ever been tempted to have breakfast, lunch, or dinner at some of the greasy fast-food restaurants dotting the highways and city landscapes?

You're not alone.

We all have at one time or another.

May I make a simple suggestion, if for any reason you're looking for a convenient way to curb your intake of fast foods?

Be strong.

Don't yield to the temptation of placing an order.

What strategies are at your disposal if you ever find yourself pinned in between two automobiles in a drive-thru restaurant?

I can think of one simple solution.

When it's safe to move your car ahead in line, heed the advice on the restaurant's signage or marquee, and yes, DRIVE THRU — without ordering food!

It's fun.

It's memorable.

It's character building.

And with a little diligence you'll save a ton of calories you didn't need to eat.

Go ahead.

Be old-fashioned.

Pack a healthy meal that you prepared at home.

Toss the Cookies—Not the Salads

One of the simplest things you can do to begin your weight loss program is to start removing certain things from your kitchen cabinets.

Have some fun.

Be creative.

Begin by placing a large plastic garbage bag directly in the middle of your kitchen floor.

Take aim.

Start launching.

Toss the "goodies," otherwise known as the problematic junk foods, directly into the center of the large plastic bag.

Fill it up, to the brim if necessary.

With the bag in hand, take a few large bold strides on your way to the trash can or Dumpster.

Don't be bashful.

Kick your heels together in celebration.

It's a big day.

Tossing cookies is a lot like getting rid of rolls and buns, you just look and feel much better when they're not hanging around.

And don't forget, healthy foods, like fruit and garden salads shouldn't be *tossed*—just mixed.

In no time you'll appreciate the benefits of having a kitchen full of healthy fresh foods.

Shop When You're Hungry

It's common knowledge that we purchase more food at the grocery store when we're walking up and down the food aisles famished and stricken with a ravenous appetite, than when we're not hungry.

Growl.

Growl.

Growl.

Shopping at the grocery store when you're hungry not only increases the number of calories in your shopping cart, but can eventually lead to more stubborn calories loitering around your waistline.

There are, however, times when you should shop when you are hungry. Be different, add a novel twist to your shopping list. Go shopping for running shoes, workout clothes, or sporting equipment when you're hungry, instead of grocery shopping when you're looking for things you don't need to eat.

Shop all you want when you're hungry. You may even burn a few of those little pesky calories while you're out on your shopping spree.

Shop.

Shop.

Walk.

Walk.

It's fun exercise.

Limit Your Consumption of TV Dinners

Where you eat can be as important as what you eat and how much you eat. What you eat and how much you eat is often influenced by WHERE you eat.

There is an important principle in real estate that affects property value. This simple principle can be summed up in just three words.

Location.

Location.

Location.

Yes, this valuable principle applies to more than real estate values, it also applies to your diet.

Where do you like to eat your meals or snacks?

In the kitchen or at your dining room table? Behind the wheel of your car cruising down the highway? At your desk? Or, are you eating your meals in front of your television set?

I like to call the meal you're eating in front of your television a TV DINNER.

Do you know how many people eat in front of their television sets?

Millions.

Studies have shown a direct relationship between the number of TV DINNERS consumed and an increased incidence of weight gain. The more you eat and the less you move, the more you will weigh.

Period.

So, breaking the TV DINNER habit may be one of the biggest steps you'll make toward losing weight.

Here's an idea.

The next time you want a TV DINNER, listen instead to your favorite music or radio station at your dining room table.

So, change channels.

Put an end to your appetite for TV DINNERS.

Avoid Frydays

Have you ever noticed that some weeks seem a little bit longer than others, while other weeks in the year seem a little shorter?

That's not unusual.

In any event, most of us would probably enjoy adding a few extra weekend days to our week or cutting out a few of those long workweek days from our schedule.

But unfortunately that's not realistic unless you're retired.

There's hope.

Actually there are certain days of the week that we can benefit from if we eliminate them from the week.

They are known as Frydays.

Frydays, and worse yet, deep-frydays, are those days during the week when you're either frying foods in fats or buying deep-fried foods at some convenience stop.

It's all the same.

Calories.

Calories.

Calories.

Pounds.

Pounds.

Pounds.

Fried foods are loaded with clingy fats that your body doesn't need any day of the week. Incidentally, it may be a great idea to also bid farewell to Sundaes as well.

Saying goodbye to fatty foods is one of the biggest steps you can take in controlling your intake of calories on any day of the week.

Here's to the rest of your week.

Hello, Monday!

Time Out

The last one to finish—wins!

The first to finish—loses!

Confused?

Don't be.

We're talking about how fast people eat.

Eating was never supposed to be a race.

Studies have shown that people have a tendency to eat less food when they eat more slowly.

Conversely, fast eaters eat more food.

Additional research studies have shown that it takes approximately 20 minutes or so for your brain to register or acknowledge that you have eaten.

Imagine how many unwanted calories you could actually consume before your brain has a chance to slow the onslaught of calories entering your body.

So, relax.

Slow down.

Lose the race.

Be the one who wins by losing, weight, that is.

Don't Move Home Plate

Losing weight is a lot like playing baseball.

It takes more than just practice, patience, and perseverance to win. It's also going to take setting very specific goals and then covering all your bases, especially home plate.

Saying that you want to lose some weight is about as vague as saying you want to swing at a few balls.

To win at losing weight, your goals or plans must be crystal clear. People who have difficulty reaching their goals usually have not taken the time to clearly visualize them.

There are eight key rules for setting goals and reshaping behavior that are presented below. Together, they have the power to help you change your behavior and help you manage your weight.

Rule 1. Identify a desire or need.

Do your goals involve personal growth, work, leisure, relationships, finances, health, fitness, or weight loss? Specific interests or desires must be identified.

Rule 2. Identify what gets in the way of changing.

Sometimes we blame other people for preventing us from accomplishing a certain goal. The truth is, we usually are our own worst interference. We don't need anyone to stop us; we can do it ourselves. How many silent conversations have you had with yourself that limit or block change in your own life?

Some people have them daily.

This private "chatterbox" can shackle you to the same old way of thinking. Every day, some people play negative tapes about doubt, insecurity, pity, and worry.

Changing this pattern requires silencing the negative chatter. Recognize what tape is playing, then eject it and insert a new, more positive voice.

Rule 3. Make sure change needs to happen.

Time is truly a precious commodity. Most people do not think about the value of time until reminded by a birthday or a deadline. Before spending valuable time designing a goal, be certain it is something truly needed. Many times we labor over things that are unimportant or we do what other people want.

Be clear about what you value. If good health is the goal, outline steps that will accomplish this. If overeating habits prevent pleasure, then the goal becomes "stop munching." A first step might be to get the junk food out of the house.

Rule 4. Goals must be specific.

It feels great to have lofty goals. Although they help us aim in the right direction, such goals can be too abstract to manage.

People who simply want to be "healthy, wealthy, and wise," need to divide these goals into specific objectives.

Tangible steps toward improving health could mean reaching a target blood pressure, cholesterol level, or resting heart rate. It also could mean specifying a desired weight or gaining freedom from medications or drugs used to treat a specific condition. Saying "NO MORE" to eating rich, fatty foods are examples of setting specific goals.

Let's say you would like to be more physically fit. Whether you want to walk upstairs without getting winded or run a marathon race, you must be specific and picture your goal in detail.

Rule 5. Prioritize goals.

Some goals are more important than others. So, they must be prioritized on the basis of need, value, and time constraints.

To help sort out each goal, classify them according to three categories: short, medium, and long-range.

Short-range goals are accomplished between today and the next several months. Deadlines are essential. Medium-range goals fall between one and several years. Both short- and medium-range goals need to be very specific. Long-range goals give overall direction and guidance and do not need to be as specific. Medium- and long-range goals are sustained and realized through the application of short-range goals.

What you do now determines what comes knocking at your door tomorrow. Your health is not an event where something is accomplished, it's a lifestyle. What you eat for breakfast, lunch and dinner, how you deal with stress, how often you exercise, and the quantity and quality of your diet all determine your health in the years to come.

Rule 6. Goals must be written down.

The best way to anchor a goal is to write it down. There is something compelling about wet ink on dry paper. Goals that are not written down are easily forgotten. They have little chance of becoming anything more than great intentions.

Every goal should be outlined in small steps and presented in a realistic and achievable format. Planning to run a six-minute mile by the end of the week is an unrealistic goal if someone is out of physical condition. Radical change in a diet also can be a little shattering. Each of us is the best judge of our abilities and can best set our own goals. The object is to turn thought into action.

Rule 7. Goals must have action behind them.

Once identified, you need to act on your goals immediately; it does not matter how much is done at first. What matters most is that you act swiftly. This might mean placing a telephone call or finding an old pair of running shoes. Digging the shoes out of the closet gets the ball rolling. Prevailing over any challenge starts with the smallest step.

Take a bold step.

Set a goal.

Then stick to it.

Whether you decide to walk, run, or be carried around the bases, make sure that you never lose sight of home plate.

Rule 8. Never give up.

The only time a goal should be abandoned is when that goal has been reevaluated and will no longer serve your best interests. If you really want something, you must put one foot in front of the other until you get there. Too many people give up just before their goals or dreams turn into reality. Keep in mind, if you give up, you surely will not succeed.

Maybees, Wannabees, Usedtobees, and Canbees

People are like bees. But we don't call them honeybees, we call them *Maybees*, *Usetobees*, *Wannabees*, and *Canbees*.

Let's first meet the *Maybees*. They're quite easy to spot because they're indecisive and unable to make decisions. The *Maybees* become paralyzed from taking action in their lives because of all the trauma and pain they have experienced from confronting agonizing choices. Incidentally, *Maybees* have not quite decided if they're going to start making any lifestyle changes.

Usetobees, "used to," but, whatever they once did, they don't do it any longer. The *Usetobees* get very little done because they spend most of their time reminiscing about the good ol' days.

The *Usetobees* have similar traits to their close cousins, the *Wannabees*. The *Wannabees* are relentless and tireless in their desire to "want to" do things, but unfortunately something always interferes with them doing so. Do these *bees* "want to" make changes to their diet and lifestyle? You bet they do!

Lastly, are the *Canbees*. They're all very active *bees* with very busy schedules. Incidentally, all these *bees* pay close attention to their lifestyles and work hard to adhere to healthy diets!

Do you know any of these *bees*, personally?

The question becomes, which *bee* are you? We have all at one time or another been one or more of these *bees*. Regardless of what kind of *bee* you presently are, or what kind of *bee* you have been in the past, the kind of *bee* you want to become is far more important to you now.

On page 185, you may want to take a challenge and discover what kind of dietary changes you're willing to make and when you're willing to start. Find a pencil or pen and use it to carefully consider your responses to the questions.

Have fun!

Getting Started

Start by doing what's necessary, then what's possible,
and suddenly you are doing the impossible.

 - Saint Francis of Assisi, 1181-1226

Seize the Moment

How do you begin to change your diet?

By simply starting!

Consider the encouraging thoughts of philosopher Wolfgang von Goethe. "Are you in earnest? Seize this very minute. What you can do, or dream you can, begin it, boldness has genius, power, and magic in it. Only engage, and then the mind grows heated—begin it, and the work will be completed."

It makes no difference what you want to change—begin it, and you'll make it happen. You may first want to consider exactly what you want to change about your diet. Do you want to change:

The quantity of food you eat?

The quality or type of food you eat?

The time of day or night you eat?

The number of times you eat each day?

How fast you eat?

Where you eat?

Write down your answers in detail.

Next, ask yourself when are you willing to make a commitment:

Today?

Tomorrow?

Next week?

This month?

Sometime?

Not sure—I need more time to think about it!

When you start asking specific questions, and answering those questions, then you will start getting specific results. If you have already answered some of these important questions then you have already started thinking about precisely what you WANT to change about your diet.

I Can and I Will

Let's get down to serious business.

By now, you have certainly identified certain foods, activities, and behaviors that are either good or bad for your health and waistline.

Go ahead, list them in detail.

On the last few pages of this book, list ONLY the foods, activities, and behaviors that you are willing and determined to change. Some people WANT to change certain lifestyle behaviors, but for whatever reason they're not wholeheartedly committed.

Remember, the word WANT can be a desire as weak as a wish or as strong as a commitment. Although the word WANT is often misunderstood, a good grasp of its meaning can change your diet—your weight—and your life.

For a moment, think about the various meanings and implications of the definitions of the word WANT. The word WANT can be defined as wishing, hoping, dreaming or longing for something; expressing a casual interest; having a curiosity; expressing an earnest desire; feeling a need; being determined; and, having an unwavering commitment to work toward a goal.

However determined and committed you are to making a lifestyle change, remember this thought:

As a dreamer and as a doer, you have both the freedom and the strength to shape your mind, your body, and your life to a point that reflects the boundary of your thoughts.

Whatever your plans are—believe you can and know you will.

Good luck!

And enjoy your journey.

Appendix (Physical Activity Guidelines)

Aside from the recommendation that individuals consume a nutritionally-balanced diet on a daily basis, regular physical activity on most days of the week has been determined to be important not only for good physical and mental health, but also essential in managing and controlling an individual's weight. Recently, the United States Department of Agriculture (USDA) has modified its recommendations and guidelines for exercise and physical activity for Americans.

In essence, according to the USDA *Dietary Guidelines for Americans 2005*, most adults should engage in at least 30 minutes of moderate-intensity physical activity, above usual activity, on most days of the week, in order to reduce the risk of developing chronic diseases in adulthood. In order to better manage body weight and reduce the possibility of weight gain in adulthood, the USDA recommends approximately 60 minutes of moderate to vigorous-intensity physical activity or at least 60 to 90 minutes of moderate-intensity physical activity most days of the week, while not exceeding their energy intake requirements. Dividing up the time of physical activity during the day can be a personal decision, but at least 10-minute intervals are recommended.

Although only an estimate, examples of moderate-intensity physical activity may include activities such as walking, mowing the lawn, and recreational bicycling. Examples of vigorous-intensity physical activity may include activities such as running, swimming, and aerobic dancing. You may want to do further research in this field to develop a better understanding of estimated caloric expenditures for various physical activities. Incidentally, most exercise physiology books are an excellent place to find tables and charts displaying a wide range of physical activities and their corresponding estimated caloric expenditures.

In addition to the general adult population, those people in a specific population group which includes, but is not limited to, children, adolescents, pregnant women, breast feeding women, older adults, or individuals with any medical, physical, health, or dietary condition that may require any treatment, medical assistance, or supervision, should not only study and discuss the USDA *Dietary Guidelines for Americans 2005* for their specific group with their licensed physician, but also consult with their licensed physician before accepting and engaging in the recommendations of any group, agency, or organization.

Remember, assistance involving any aspect of personal health, fitness, and diet should be addressed by a licensed physician or certified/qualified health care professional in the field. The author and publisher strongly encourage the reader to always consult with your physician before making any decisions that may affect your health, particularly if you have any medical, physical, health, or dietary condition that may require any treatment, medical assistance, or supervision.

From all of us at HealthSpan Communications, we hope you have enjoyed the thoughts and messages expressed in this book . . . and have in some special way been touched, inspired, and enlightened.

Please visit our website at **smallest*things*.com** for all the latest books, digitally mastered CD audiobooks, and other new products.

The first audio CD set released in the series:
The Smallest Things Make the Biggest Difference.®

ISBN 978-0-9643673-5-7 $18   2 CD Set (2 Hours Indexed)
Narrated by the author and artfully orchestrated to beautiful music.

The first book released in the series:
The Smallest Things Make the Biggest Difference.®

ISBN 978-0-9643673-2-6 $12.95   160 pages

*"**The Smallest Things Make the Biggest Difference** is a little gem.
Dr. Haring collects a gallery of profound thoughts and insights into
the human character, creating a collage of very compelling stories
and quotes. This book is worth your time to sit and read."*

Kenneth Blanchard, Ph.D., Co-author
#1 National Bestseller
The One-Minute Manager

*"Discover the miracles that can come out of life's simplicities.
Dr. Haring will inspire you to be more, give more, take more
chances, and ultimately be more alive."*

Anthony Robbins, Author
#1 National Bestseller
Awaken the Giant Within

*"A wonderful collection of positive and refreshing observations
of life. An uplifting read for anyone searching for an oasis amidst
life's many distractions."*

John Gray, Ph.D., Author
#1 National Bestseller
Men are From Mars, Women are From Venus

Notes

Notes